FACILITATION
made easy

BST

FACILITATION
made easy

Practical Tips to Improve Meetings and Workshops

3rd edition

ESTHER CAMERON

KOGAN PAGE

London and Sterling, VA

Publisher's note

Every possible effort has been made to ensure that the information contained in this book is accurate at the time of going to press, and the publishers and authors cannot accept responsibility for any errors or omissions, however caused. No responsibility for loss or damage occasioned to any person acting, or refraining from action, as a result of the material in this publication can be accepted by the editor, the publisher or the author.

First published in 1998
Second edition 2001
Third edition 2005

Kogan Page Limited
120 Pentonville Road
London N1 9JN
United Kingdom
www.kogan-page.co.uk

Kogan Page US
22883 Quicksilver Drive
Sterling VA 20166-2012
USA

ISBN 0 7494 4351 0

British Library Cataloguing in Publication Data

A CIP record for this book is available from the British Library

---

Library of Congress Cataloging-in-Publication Data

Cameron, Esther.
    Facilitation made easy : practical tips to improve meetings and workshops
/ Esther Cameron. -- 3rd ed.
        p. cm.
    Includes bibliographical references and index.
    ISBN 0-7494-4351-0
1. Group facilitation 2. Employees--Training of. I. Title.
HM751.C36 2005
658.4'036--dc22
                                        2005014933

Typeset by Jean Cussons Typesetting, Diss, Norfolk
Printed and bound in Great Britain by Creative Print and Design (Wales), Ebbw Vale

Contents

Preface

In organizations today, traditional management skills are becoming outmoded. Until recently, managers have been encouraged to run things in a very linear fashion. Work was mainly done with a fixed team on a fixed project, and management involved setting objectives, planning, delegating and monitoring.

Today's manager cannot 'manage' in the same way. Fierce competition, globalization, flatter organizations, home-working and the rise of knowledge working all go together to create a new climate. People do not work in fixed teams at one site any more, and the tasks are far from predictable or linear.

Many organizations are responding to this new climate by encouraging their managers and their key staff to pick up new skills to cope with the new challenges. Facilitation skills have now become vital not only for the successful manager, but for the successful business consultant and the successful technical specialist. Peter Senge of MIT says 'Today everyone in business is into "teams", but learning how to "think together" involves very high-level skills that few managers have.'

When groups of people get together in today's organizations, time is like gold dust. We all have to learn how to use this precious time to help people to think imaginatively, communicate clearly, learn from each other and come up with workable solutions to problems.

I know from experience that facilitation skills can be mastered by anyone who wants to learn. I have seen engineers, computer experts, production supervisors and old-school managers all grasp the skills and fly with them. It is tremendously liberating to discover how to run a really enjoyable, stimulating, purposeful workshop. Say goodbye to glum faces and folded arms!

My mission is to bring facilitation skills out into the open. These skills are not the preserve of organizational development consultants and business psychologists. I wanted to write a book that debunked facilitation and made it accessible. I believe strongly that anyone can do it, given a bit of clear instruction and room to practise.

So what is in the book? Chapter 1 introduces facilitation by explaining what a facilitated workshop is for and discussing what is expected of the facilitator.

Chapter 2, by way of setting the scene, gives some useful psychological background to the way groups behave. Chapters 3, 4, 5 and 6 home in on the key workshop lifecycle activities. These chapters explain how to plan, conduct and follow-up after a facilitated workshop.

Chapter 7 acknowledges the fact that facilitated workshops do not exist in a vacuum, and addresses a range of issues surrounding facilitated workshops, such as change programmes and the use of external facilitators. Chapter 8 sets out four real life case studies to illustrate how facilitated workshops are used, the problems that can arise and the achievements that can be made.

Chapter 9 covers two special workshop cases: top team sessions and cross-cultural groups. I use cross-cultural in the widest sense.

Too busy to read the book? Don't worry as Chapter 11 gives you the facilitator's complete checklist which will help to ensure that you have covered the necessary ground.

The STOP AND THINK! sections throughout the book encourage the reader to think about the material rather than just skim through it and Chapter 9 gives the author's responses to the STOP AND THINK! questions. Chapter 10 examines the impact of virtual teams and how to conduct virtual meetings.

I would like to acknowledge the clients and colleagues with whom I have developed and run facilitation skills training courses and facilitated workshops over the past few years. Their questions, comments and real life examples have enabled me to put this book together. I would like also to thank Duncan Cameron for his consistently good-natured support and for his particularly perceptive comments. Thanks also go to Louise Overy for her excellent eye for detail and to Steve Summers for his ability to weed out my errors in logic! Caroline Coard also deserves credit for planting the facilitation seed in my mind.

I hope the book proves useful and I would be very pleased to hear how you get on with your workshops. You can reach me at any time of the day or night on: esther@cameronchange.co.uk

CHAPTER 1

Introducing facilitation

What is a committee? A group of the unwilling, picked from the unfit to do the unnecessary.
Richard Harkness

Meetings have a bad reputation in today's organizations. People often see them as frustrating, lengthy, dominated by the wrong people and an unnecessary diversion from the real work. Why do we stick with this stultifying format, when it is obviously not working? Why do we carry on running our organizations via a series of ineffectual, sleep-inducing committee meetings?

Of course effective meetings do occur, but they are short, purposeful and usually fairly select. However, there are many occasions in organizations when there is a need to involve more people than just the key players. The question is, how do you involve a large number of people in a decision making process, get their ideas and opinions, and gain their commitment without causing immense frustration or boring them to tears?

This first chapter begins to answer this question by explaining what a facilitated workshop is, what it can achieve and what is expected of the facilitator. The reader has a chance to assess his or her facilitation style, and a quiz is provided (see page 7) to home in on some of the key principles and beliefs surrounding facilitation. The final section of this chapter introduces the workshop lifecycle, which is a useful reference point for the rest of the book.

What is a facilitated workshop?

A facilitated workshop is a method of allowing a group of people to work together to achieve a specific outcome. The beauty of a facilitated workshop is that everyone is encouraged to contribute, everyone gets a feeling of involvement and there are real, demonstrable outcomes. This kind of workshop can be used to address specific work problems, collect requirements for computer systems, evaluate products, build company vision, discuss company strategy or address key company issues. There are countless other applications of facilitated workshops; the outcome may be radically different, but the basic process is the same.

A group of 12 is ideal for a facilitated workshop as it gives the right balance between intimacy and liveliness. However, a workshop can theoretically run with any number of people, although anything smaller than five or larger than 15 requires a highly skilled facilitator to retain order, interest and direction.

Workshops can last anything from half a day up to several days. Half day and one day workshops work well if the facilitator is well-prepared, assertive, and well-versed in the use of structured discussion tools. Longer workshops of two days and over require a very high level of facilitation skill to run successfully, as the group dynamics and concentration levels become more complex and varied.

There are a few simple rules and principles for running facilitated workshops.

- The workshop must have a clear purpose.
- Participants attend because they have something to contribute, not simply because they represent departmental interests.
- The workshop must run according to a pre-circulated agenda which outlines a broad structure for the workshop, with some flexibility built in.
- The workshop must aim for specific outcomes, and those outcomes must be carefully recorded.
- Everyone must be included in the discussion and openness should be encouraged.
- The workshop must be deliberately made interesting and stimulating to encourage contributions.
- Participants must be encouraged to listen to each other, and to understand each other's views.
- The facilitator must be well-informed, but unbiased.
- The workshop must be part of a larger process and everyone must be kept informed of progress.

The facilitator's role and style

A workshop facilitator is someone who helps a group of people to achieve an agreed aim, by involving everyone present. The facilitator's style should be unbiased and non-manipulative, remaining in control without being overpowering.

This role differs from that of chairperson at a meeting. Typically a chaired meeting focuses on reviewing progress and agreeing actions by working through a strict agenda. The chairperson's task is to get items efficiently agreed and to set specific actions. The facilitator's role is much more about opening things up for discussion in a stimulating way, getting ideas into the open and helping the group to listen to each other, further its knowledge and thus make informed decisions. Actions may be set, but they are a by-product of the process rather than a specific goal.

So what are the key aspects of the facilitator's role? These are:

- getting a clear workshop aim;
- ensuring that the right participants are encouraged to attend;
- researching the topic;
- preparing an agenda for participants and sending this out to them well before the workshop;
- preparing the workshop structure introducing the workshop including everyone in the discussion;
- making the workshop stimulating;
- questioning what is said;
- building on what is said;
- using facilitation tools to move the discussion along;
- recording what goes on (or making sure that someone does this);
- recording any actions agreed;
- ensuring good quality follow-up after the workshop (see Chapter 6).

Every facilitator has a natural preferred style. Consider for a moment what your preferred style might be. Your preferred style will depend on your past experiences, personality, habitual ways of thinking and level of confidence in a group situation. Most people find that they need to make one or two changes to their natural style in order to facilitate effectively.

Figure 1.1 shows three useful bi-polar scales which will help you to examine your own preferred style. Each scale represents a continuum which stretches from one extreme to the other. Most people place them-selves roughly half-way between the centre point and one extreme.

The pros (+) and cons (-) of each style are listed in Figure 1.1 to help you identify areas where improvement might be made.

ACTIVE
Enthusiastic (+)
Stimulating (+)
Talks too much (-)
Gives own opinions (-)

REFLECTIVE
Thoughtful (+)
Gives people time (+)
Pace too slow (-)
Too much silence (-)

THEORETICAL
Creative (+)
Builds on ideas for the future (+)
Not pragmatic (-)
May be seen as woolly by participants (-)

FACT BASED
Practical (+)
Strong on solving problems (+)
May not value creative ideas (-)
May not look ahead (-)

AGGRESSIVE
Time managed well (+)

Pre-defined topics covered (+)

Little flexibility in discussion topics (-)
Highly directive (-)

PASSIVE
Group has a feeling of control (+)
Lots of flexibility in the discussion (+)
Weak controls on time (-)
Not directive at all – can seem aimless (-)

Figure 1.1 *Preferred facilitation styles*

Active–reflective scale

If you are an *active* person, you prefer doing to thinking, and like to be working and interacting with other people, with plenty of discussion and activity. When an active person runs a workshop, he or she will be energetic and stimulating, but may run the risk of talking too much and failing to allow enough time for thought or discussion.

If you are a *reflective* person, you prefer reflecting to acting. You may be a creative thinker or a careful planner and enjoy working alone or with one or two others with plenty of time for discussion and thought. When a reflective person runs a workshop, there is a lot of time to discuss and reflect. However, he or she may not reach the required levels of stimulation because the discussion progresses too slowly and the facilitator allows periods of silence when he or she should be responding to what is said.

Theoretical–fact based scale

If you are a *theoretical* person, you look for patterns and possibilities and tend to be oriented towards the future. A theoretical facilitator is good at building up abstract ideas about the future, but may lack the required focus on today's problems.

Conversely, *fact based* people are what works now. The fact based facilitator has the reverse profile. He or she is very concerned about the practical application of ideas, but will put less emphasis on creative possibilities for the future.

Aggressive–passive scale

This third continuum concerns the facilitator's degree of aggressive or passive behaviour. This behaviour will depend on how you react emotionally and instinctively to the situation of being in front of a group of people. If you find this situation stressful (and many people do), you will tend towards one of two instinctive responses: fight or flight. This means you will either tend to dominate the group aggressively, or you will tend passively to allow the group to run things themselves.

Aggressive facilitators dictate the agenda and control progress tightly, reigning people back in if they stray off the agenda. This means that although the workshop keeps to schedule, participants may become frustrated and angry because they are not allowed to finish what they see as important discussions. Under the regime of the aggressive facilitator, important issues that are raised during the workshop but were not foreseen cannot be aired.

Passive facilitators allow the group to discuss whatever they want, and tend to back down from their original structure if challenged. This approach has great flexibility and may provide some fun for the participants, however, the workshop may seem aimless, and frustrating; time may be wasted talking around in circles, never moving on.

After you have read and understood the descriptions for each style, place a mark at the point of each scale where you see yourself. Reflect on the pros and cons of your natural preferred style and think about the improvements that you might need to make to develop your facilitation style.

What a facilitated workshop can do (and can't do!)

Facilitated workshops are good for generating ideas, involving people, getting a wide view on a topic, gaining commitment to courses of action, selecting preferred options, making simple decisions and building teams.

They are not at all useful for giving surprises, changing people's views, persuading people, making complex decisions, focusing on individuals, giving people information (unless this is packaged with another activity from the above list) or dictating behaviour.

Thus they are not at all good for any of the examples below, all of which unfortunately came from real life workshops:

- explaining a redundancy programme;
- getting people to understand the management point of view;
- persuading a group of technicians that the existing planning policy is right;
- making a complex decision about policy for overseas staff;
- finding out who are the weak members of the team;
- informing people of changes to plan;
- telling people how to act in front of clients.

However, these issues could be tackled with a workshop if they were reframed as below:

- how to cope with a redundancy programme;
- getting people's feedback on the management point of view;
- asking a group of technicians to review the planning policy;

- getting data about and examining the key issues surrounding overseas staff;
- identifying the strengths and weaknesses of the team, and creating a plan of action;
- asking people to consider the pros and cons of a particular change of plan;
- asking people to say what resources and training they might need to enable them to change their methods of working to a particular specification.

Pre-set conclusions are an absolute no-no for workshops. Manipulative facilitators are usually fairly transparent to the participants. You will be found out somewhere along the way, and you will probably damage relationships in the long term. Why not be brave, and tell people what you have decided? Allow people to question your reasoning, but do not pretend that consultation is a necessary part of the process when you have made the decision already.

Complex tasks, such as drawing up a business plan or modelling a complicated business process cannot be made by a large group. The largest group of people that can sensibly decide on a complex issue is four. Large groups can serve only to gauge feeling and identify preferred ideas or solutions. It is a waste of time to try to get 12 people to agree a course of action.

Test your attitude to facilitation

This short quiz will help you to think over some of your ideas about facilitation. Complete the questionnaire, then read on to compare your responses with the author's.

Please read each of the following statements in turn. Circle *True* if you agree with the statement; circle *False* if you disagree.

1. Facilitating a workshop is the same as chairing a meeting   True/False

2. If you don't like doing presentations, you can't facilitate   True/False

3. If workshop participants don't contribute, it's their own lookout   True/False

4. People who don't contribute to a workshop should
    be asked direct questions to make them contribute   True/False

5. The facilitator's opinion isn't important   True/False

6. The looser the agenda the better   True/False

7. The facilitator should make sure that the workshop
    runs to time   True/False

8. Subject experts should be given the most airtime
    during a workshop   True/False

9. The facilitator should make sure that when one
    person is talking everyone else is silent   True/False

10. Follow-up after a workshop is nothing to do with
    the facilitator   True/False

11. It's OK to give the agenda out at the workshop
    rather than before   True/False

12. A facilitator should be good at listening and
    questioning   True/False

13. A facilitator should be unbiased   True/False

14. It's OK for the facilitator to know very little about
    the subject area   True/False

15. Facilitated workshops are just talking shops which
    rarely add value to the business   True/False

Now read through the author's responses.

Facilitating a workshop is the same as chairing a meeting   False

Chairing a meeting involves following a set agenda and ensuring that
decisions are reached. Facilitation involves much more stimulation,
involvement and flexibility. Whereas a chairperson is there to control
and mediate, the facilitator is there to stimulate and direct. A facilitated
workshop can be much more responsive to the group's idea about what
is important and should be designed to have some flexibility within an
overall structure.

If you don't like doing presentations, you can't facilitate   False

People mistakenly believe that facilitation is the same as presentation. The best way to get people thinking and contributing at a meeting is to give them clear relevant problems to discuss. Presentations may be entertaining, but they allow the audience to remain passive. The secret of good facilitation is to stimulate the group into constructive action, and this can be done with minimal presentation skills.

Of course, it helps if you feel comfortable up on your feet in front of a group, as you will be on show, but this is only part of the battle.

If workshop participants don't contribute, it's their own lookout False

If people do not contribute, it is for a specific reason. See the next point for some suggestions on this. Your job is to make sure that everyone contributes. Why invite them to the meeting if you do not want to hear what they have to say? I regularly hear managers complaining that their staff will not raise issues in an open forum. Even though staff may care very deeply and hold very strong views they still may not speak out because they have learnt that putting their heads above the parapet is unwise. Managers need to find ways of creating a more open environment, through better listening, or ways within workshops of assessing views anonymously. Read on to find out how to do this!

People who don't contribute to a workshop should be asked direct questions to make them contribute   False

People who do not contribute hold back for a reason. This may be through shyness, lack of knowledge of the topic, nervousness in front of seniors, annoyance, anger or disinterest. It is not your job to decide whether or not that reason is legitimate; it is your job as a facilitator to get everyone to contribute. Shyness can be overcome by using smaller groups to discuss specific topics. Annoyance and anger should be addressed privately during a break. You can be sure that asking a direct question in front of a large group will only serve to magnify the original problem.

The facilitator's opinion isn't important   True

The facilitator should question what is said, tackle inconsistencies and make sure that what is said is clear to everyone. You should resist giving your own opinions on a topic for two reasons. The first is that facilitating is a hard enough job to do without having to take part in the discussion as well. The second is that the role of facilitator brings with it a measure of influence, so your views may carry undue weight and may skew the discussion in an unhelpful way. However, you can use your knowledge of relevant facts to provide stimulating challenges to what has been said.

The looser the agenda the better   Partly True

It is important that the agenda is neither too loose nor too tight. An agenda that is too loose may seem aimless and frustrating for participants, whereas an agenda that is too tight may not give the participants a chance to spend time discussing unforeseen important issues.

The facilitator should make sure that the workshop runs to time True

Running over time at the end of a workshop is unforgivable. It is insulting to participants, who probably have many other calls on their time. It is a common error made by facilitators from the 'free and easy' school, who believe that whatever the group wants to discuss is OK by them. A more directive approach is needed, which sets out a broad-brush structure with a timescale to match. At the other end of the spectrum, it may be tempting to over control the discussion. You should not be timing discussion down to 5-, 10- or even 15- minute blocks, but rather look at half-hour blocks. This may seem daunting at first, but will become more comfortable with experience. Novice facilitators may need to focus on 20-minute blocks for comfort's sake.

Subject experts should be given the most airtime during a workshop False

It may be useful to have subject experts present, but it may be necessary to control them if they are very vocal. The object of the workshop is to get views from everyone rather than to let any one person dominate the discussion. Subject experts should be recognized for their special knowledge, and can be usefully included by being asked to verify facts, or to add their comments once everyone else has had a chance to speak.

The facilitator should make sure that when one person is talking everyone else is silent   True

Group discussions fall apart when splinter groups start to have their own private conversations. Although this may be a good sign, indicating that people are interested in the topic, the facilitator needs to make sure that participants listen to each other. This means being quiet while others speak. Groups of five and over can only function well if there is a strong facilitator ensuring both participating and listening. The facilitator should steer clear of the Jean Brodie technique of treating the participants like naughty school children with a brusque 'Shush!'. This will only encourage more 'naughty' behaviour. Try to treat the participants in an adult fashion by pre-empting this problem with a clear set of discussion ground rules agreed by the group at the start of the workshop.

Follow-up after a workshop is nothing to do with the facilitator
False

The workshop is normally part of a larger consultative process, which the facilitator should be aware of. This process should involve telling participants what will happen after the workshop, and giving them a short report, which shows how the results of the workshop were presented to the rest of the organization. Any actions resulting from the workshop should be communicated to the participants, together with clear reasons for any decision not to act. If this is not done, people will probably assume that the workshop did not result in any action and was therefore of little direct use. This will make future workshops less popular and may result in high levels of cynicism. Although as the facilitator, you may not be specifically charged with this responsibility, you should treat it as part of making the workshop work, and should advise your sponsor of the importance of good follow-up.

It's OK to give the agenda out at the workshop rather than before
False

Avoid this by preparing in advance. If you decide to run a workshop, this implies that you need constructive contributions from the participants, which will often require some research or general cogitation before the workshop. If participants receive a clear agenda, they can think about the topics beforehand, otherwise they arrive cold.

A facilitator should be good at listening and questioning   True

Listening and questioning skills are much more important for facilitation than presentation skills. The facilitator needs to be both stimulating and challenging so that the best ideas are captured, and the best solutions sought. This can only be done through keen questioning and avid listening.

A facilitator should be unbiased   True

The facilitator is there to gather the views of the group and encourage discussion. An unbiased approach is essential. Any bias will be picked up on by the group, and may skew their responses or may cause them to withhold contributions because they think the decision has already been made. If you do hold strong views, you may wish to put them on the table first, backing them up with facts. Then you must open these views up for discussion in an unbiased way: Do not enter a workshop as facilitator with your mind made up. This will be a pointless exercise for you and a frustrating one for the participants.

It is OK for the facilitator to know very little about the subject area   False

No, it is not OK. Facilitators who are brought in simply to arbitrate and then write up any decisions on the flipchart do not add value. The facilitator should be familiar with at least some aspects of the area under discussion. This enables the facilitator to understand quickly the language used, and to question what is said.

Facilitated workshops are just talking shops which rarely add value to the business   True and False

I'm afraid this is sometimes true, although it shouldn't be. The usual problems are: bad planning; lack of open discussion; poor decision making; poor workshop reporting; poor follow-up; and an inability to take the views of those lower down the tree seriously. Because of these problems, workshops have sometimes gained a bad reputation.

Failing to take the views of those lower down the tree seriously is one of the most common reasons for failure of facilitated workshops. But as Gary Hamel, Visiting Professor of Strategic and International Management at the London Business School, wrote recently 'if you draw an organizational pyramid with senior management at the top... Where in that pyramid do you find the least genetic diversity when it comes to thinking in radically different ways about the future of an industry?' Senior managers have to learn to listen to the more junior members of staff.

The workshop lifecycle

The facilitated workshop lifecycle illustrated in Figure 1.2 highlights the important stages in the workshop's life. People tend to focus on planning and running the workshop, but often forget to define the workshop purpose or follow up afterwards. The facilitator needs to be aware that problems may occur at any one of the four stages defined for the workshop lifecycle, and that the workshop needs to be carefully shepherded around its lifecycle.

All four stages in the workshop lifecycle will be discussed in detail in the following chapters.

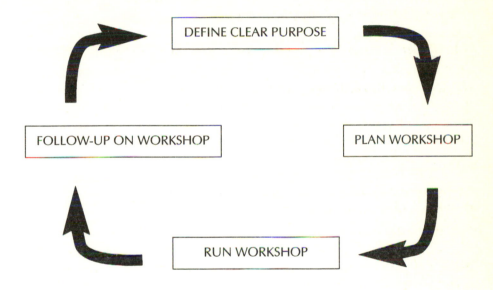

Figure 1.2 *The workshop lifecycle*

STOP AND THINK!

Here are some questions, which may help you to reflect on and digest this chapter. Notice that if you are an active type of person, your instinct will be to skip this bit and press on with the next chapter!

Question 1

You are an internal human resources consultant for Drring Tele-communications Ltd. The Operations Manager has asked you to run a workshop for his senior technical people, which he has called 'Lets Talk'. He wants you to get them to see that their problems are all because they refuse to talk to each other, and to work on ways of talking more frequently. How do you react?

Question 2

You have just attended a workshop on the requirements for the next generation of Management Information Systems for your organization. The external facilitator was very lively and came up with a long list of suggestions for what the system could do. The discussion involved only one or two participants, who questioned her suggestions and found that she did not quite grasp what you actually do in your organization. Most participants failed to participate at all, and the output was simply the list that the facilitator had generated with half the items crossed off.

What went wrong? How could things be improved for the next workshop in this series, which will be on a similar topic, but for your sister company?

CHAPTER 2

The psychology of groups

When people are thrust together in a workshop group, they do not behave as they would in a conversational or small group situation. If the facilitator understands some of the natural habits of groups, he or she maximizes the chance of the workshop running successfully.

If you are only running short, half-day workshops, you can probably get by with just a rudimentary understanding of the psychology of groups. When groups stay together for two or more days, group processes kick in and start to affect how well the workshop runs.

This chapter sets out to explain the reasons behind group behaviour and to identify what to watch out for when facilitating a workshop. Useful ideas are given on how to handle different aspects of group behaviour in a workshop situation.

Social behaviour

Human beings are social animals. We survive the challenges of the outside world by building up complex networks of relationships and coalitions. Some of these social relationships are purely one-to-one, and some are as part of a group. Humans have innate social needs, which means that although we may strive to develop an individual identity, we also want to belong.

This need to belong translates into particular types of behaviour in group situations. Think about your behaviour when you are alone or with very close friends, and compare this to your behaviour in a variety of group situations. What differences are there?

Typical differences cited are:

- 'I might take my shoes off when I am at a friend's house, but never at work.'

- 'I eat my sandwiches much quicker, and far less politely when no one is looking.'
- 'I am less guarded in my criticism of others when with close friends. In a group situation, I would watch what I say, especially in front of the senior managers.'
- 'I would be unlikely to speak out first on a burning issue. I would wait to see if others thought the same before chipping in.'
- 'If most of the key players in the team supported a line of action with which I disagreed, I might decide to keep quiet about my views, just for a quiet life.'
- 'I would pursue an issue so far, but if a significant number of the others in the team disagreed, I would tend to concede the point.'

The first two examples identified in the list above are essentially fairly trivial. However, the last three examples show how the group situation can mitigate against openness and honesty. It is therefore very useful for the facilitator to understand this aspect of group behaviour in order to facilitate effectively.

As illustrated above, the group situation created by a facilitated workshop can be fraught with problems with openness and honesty. This effect is present whatever the group, but is particularly strong when people of different status levels are mixed together.

Solomon Asch's experiment, carried out back in 1951, illustrates this point very well. He was interested in how easy or difficult it was for a person to stick to his or her own opinion, when the rest of the group held a different opinion and whether the status levels of the group members made any difference to this effect.

Asch constructed an experiment, which studies conformance behaviour. He gathered together a group of seven subjects. However, there was only one true volunteer in the subject group; the other six people were associates of Asch. The group was presented with a display, which allowed them to compare the length of one line with a selection of four other lines of varying length. The task was to select which of the four lines matched the length of the original line. Asch's associates had been told beforehand to choose one particular line, which was clearly not the same length as the original line.

This experiment was repeated with several volunteer subjects, using a variety of sets of lines. On hearing the views of others in the group, only 25 per cent of the volunteer subjects consistently stuck to their own views; 30 per cent went along with the incorrect views of the group and

45 per cent varied between sticking to their guns and going along with the group. The conformity effect was noted to be significantly stronger when the volunteer perceived himself or herself to be of lower status than the rest of the group.

The facilitator needs to be aware of the pressure some participants feel to conform to the group view, or particularly to the views of managers and senior staff. Sometimes this is hard for facilitators to understand. One manager at a recent Facilitation Skills Workshop told us a story about his Problem Solving Workshop.

> I set this workshop up specifically to address the concerns that two of the more junior members of staff had about the new organizational changes. I knew they were very upset about several issues and I was intending to support them in solving these problems. However, when we ran the workshop, the more senior members of the team spoke positively about the changes, and the junior members just went along with it all. I was amazed. Had they changed their minds? Of course not, they both resigned a couple of months later. But why did they not speak out when they had the chance?

Why should this be? Asch's experiment gives us the answer. There is pressure to conform in a group situation, and people who perceive themselves to be of low status within the group feel this pressure more acutely. Therefore junior team members may go along with the views of more senior people when in a group situation, while holding radically different views in private.

So how can a workshop facilitator get around these problems? If you are the manager of the team, you will have to be especially careful when you tackle very sensitive issues. You can try following the ideas outlined below or you may want to consider using an external facilitator.

The first way of relaxing people and avoiding any formal atmosphere, which might build up in a workshop, is to ensure that people get a chance to introduce themselves at the start. This helps to make everyone feel much more comfortable, and ensures that everyone is very clear about who is present.

If senior managers are present and there are difficult issues to tackle, be aware that the less senior members of the group are likely to temper what they say. This depends on group behaviour norms (see page 20) which are usually such that more senior people in the organization have more power, and are rarely challenged in public. Use secret suggestion techniques and secret voting techniques to circumvent these difficulties. Secret suggestion is simply achieved by asking individuals to write down their key issues, and hand them to you anonymously. This can be done before or during the workshop. Secret voting involves collecting people's votes on the importance or urgency of various issues in a confident way. This technique is described in Chapter 3.

Types of group

A facilitated workshop involves getting a group of people together to think, discuss and interact. How do people behave in this particular type of group situation? It is useful to reflect on the three main types of group to which we belong, to gain a better understanding of the behaviour of participants at a facilitated workshop.

The *family group* is the most important and formative group in our lives. In the family group, we learn acceptable ways of behaving, and we learn that conforming to the accepted ways of behaving can earn us rewards. For instance, a child who eats up his first course 'nicely' may be given extra pudding. The family also gives us our first experience of performing a role within a group. Children explore the meaning of various family roles through play by pretending to be 'mum' or 'dad'. This all prepares us for our membership of adult groups in later life, in terms of conforming and taking on roles. People at facilitated workshops do find themselves taking on particular roles (see page 21).

The *work group* becomes very important in adult life. This is the long-term, well-established group or organization to which a person belongs which helps to sustain his or her livelihood, and defines his or her status and social standing in life. The manager of the workgroup is a very important figure, as are the informal shapers of opinion; these people establish the pattern of behaviour in the group, influencing what is acceptable and what is not, and helping to define who lives where in the pecking order (see page 19).

Increasingly, people who attend my workshops say they do not really belong to a permanent workgroup as they move rapidly from project to project, establishing brief *ad hoc* relationships as they go. I meet many others who operate as independent consultants. These people tend to survive by establishing a loose network of contacts who rarely all meet together, so cannot be described as a workgroup. Thus modern work patterns often result in lone or transient working and groups are much more diffuse as a result.

Despite the potential isolation of working life, the social animal in us still needs the stimulation and warmth of the group, which means that when people do actually meet in groups, the potential for success is enormous. Be aware that lone workers may not be well practised in the art of fitting in with a group and making the odd compromise, so a facilitated workshop full of independent consultants is a potential battleground of egos. Strong ground rules, plenty of relevant activity and some fairly directive facilitation will help to circumvent this problem.

The *ad hoc* group is the most common group to which adults belong. This is a group that comes together for a limited time for the purpose of completing a specific task. Facilitated workshop groups fall into this category, as do training groups and project groups.

The longer the *ad hoc* group spends together, the more it begins to resemble a work group as described above, with group norms, pecking order and fixed roles. The small *ad hoc* group of three to four people may remain relatively free of leadership struggles for a limited period, provided it is comprised of equals. However, a workshop group of five people and over will begin to exhibit work group tendencies, and to sort out its pecking order (see below). Workshops comprising colleagues from an existing work group will operate under the rules established by the original work group. Do not expect to be able to change these rules in two days or less.

Pecking order

As we are social animals, our social standing is of key importance to us, much as we may wish ourselves to be above such things. The expression 'pecking order' comes from the social behaviour of hens, in which formal rules govern which hen is allowed to peck with other hens. Likewise, groups of five people or more like to establish some form of pecking order or hierarchy of importance. Well-established groups will already have sorted out their pecking order, so are less prone to leadership struggles. Homogeneous groups of equals are also less trouble in this respect.

However, for one-off workshop groups of at least one day in length, this is a real issue. The way groups work out the pecking order depends on a complex combination of level of experience, status in an organization, knowledge, deftness of argument and body language. The workshop introduction is a good way of getting a lot of this information out into the open and helping to make people feel comfortable. It is important to help people to get to know each other quickly because if the participants are busy establishing their pecking order, they are not busy thinking creatively and constructively.

Group norms

A group norm refers to the accepted way of behaving in a group. This concept starts in the family group, in which children learn what kind of behaviour is acceptable in society at large. This would refer to simple behaviours such as having good table manners, remembering not to drop rubbish in the street, or saying please and thank you (especially in the UK).

Work groups establish group norms, which govern what is acceptable, and what is not. For instance some work groups are very tolerant of bad language, while others are not. Some support high performers, others ostracize them. Some are highly consultative, while others are used to being told what to do. A workshop comprising members from an existing work group will tend to follow the existing norms of that group. If the leader of the group is not present, there is more chance of establishing a new set of norms. So, for instance, if the work group normally functions by receiving instructions without questions, the facilitator will have to explain that the workshop is about questioning instructions, or coming up with a new set of instructions, and that this is allowed and encouraged.

In a group of mixed status which includes, for example, senior managers mixed with technical staff, the technical staff will already have some idea of what it is acceptable to say and do in front of the senior managers and what is not acceptable. Likewise, the senior managers will have a fairly fixed idea of how to act in front of technical staff.

The facilitator has to work within these norms, and cannot expect to override them. If technical staff have strong views about the senior management, but do not feel comfortable being critical in an open forum, no amount of exhortations to be 'open and honest' will get them to state these views in front of the senior managers. The only way is to use techniques that allow participants to suggest ideas anonymously.

The facilitated workshop comprising equals who do not really know each other can establish its own norms. The facilitator should encourage the group to do this by setting workshop ground rules at the start of the workshop covering areas such as levels of honesty and amount of airtime per individual. The facilitator can speed this process up by suggesting a list, which the group can add to or modify (see Chapter 4 for a possible list).

Coalitions

Our closest primate cousin, the chimpanzee, can teach us a thing or two about coalitions. Chimpanzees spend at least 20 per cent of the day grooming each other. Why waste all this valuable feeding time? Anthropologists believe, through observing chimpanzees, that this activity strengthens coalitions between individual chimps, as chimps come more readily to the defence of recent grooming partners. Likewise, in human groups, individuals have a need to form coalitions as an extra defence should they get into trouble with powerful individuals within the larger group. This is very much a belt and braces approach!

In a workshop situation, people may begin to form coalitions in twos or threes, or these may already be well-established. As facilitator, you will notice this happening when two people are continually sharing comments under their breath or laughing together or sitting very close with legs crossed towards each other (see body language section). Other signs include always espousing the same views and supporting each other. This becomes a problem when the chattering disturbs other group members, or when the duo or trio becomes intransigent. The facilitator can circumvent this problem in one or both of the following ways:

- ask participants to sit next to people they do not know right at the start of the workshop;
- split the coalition up for the next workshop activity.

Typical roles

In a facilitated workshop of at least one day, you may notice people gravitating towards particular workshop roles such as the following:

- *Leader* – One of the groups may emerge as spokesperson for the group. The facilitator should respect this role. If the emerging leader has a consultative style, then there will be no problems. If the emerging leader has a domineering style, then the majority of the other participants will tend to tacitly support the leader's views, even if they disagree in reality. Use secret voting techniques if necessary.

21

- *Adversary* – There is often one member of the group who remains in adversarial mood throughout the workshop. He or she will make a point of playing devil's advocate at every opportunity. This may be about specific points raised in the workshop or about the workshop as a whole. If the workshop is well-constructed and purposeful, this person will either come round naturally, or others in the group will ask him or her to pipe down. If not, the facilitator must make sure that any irrelevant or repetitive arguing is curtailed, possibly by having a private word with the person. The adversary should also be reminded that airtime is to be shared equally amongst the participants.

- *Harmonizer* – Someone in the group may emerge as the person whose role it is to smooth over troubled waters. This can be useful for creating a relaxed, harmonious atmosphere in cases where participants are getting worked up about irrelevant and diverting issues. However, the harmonizer can be counter-productive if people wish to air strong, relevant views. The harmonizer may have to be told to sit back while opposing views are aired, and resist the temptation to suggest that the two views are really the same, or that the problem is being addressed or will go away.

- *Joker* – The group joker may emerge over time. This person sees his or her role in the group as the provider of levity and entertainment. This may be clever humour, or self-deprecating jokes. Either is fine in moderation. The facilitator should ensure that this individual is involved and kept busy, otherwise he or she can become disruptive. If the workshop participants are finding the jokes amusing, then beware putting the joker down in front of the rest of the group. This may turn the group against you.

- *Outlier* – The outlier appears in many, many workshops. He or she begins by holding different views. The person may also dress differently, work differently and act differently from the other workshop participants. If the outlier does not warm to the workshop topic and does not let himself or herself get involved, then this person may become more and more isolated as the workshop progresses. This behaviour is probably the habit of a lifetime for this person, so the facilitator should not worry too much about whether the outlier is contributing or not. Gentle persuasion is quite adequate, preferably in private, together with some probing questions about the way that the workshop is going. But beware! – outliers have a habit of consuming vast amounts of facilitator effort for very little return.

Common goals

Work group members need a common goal if they are to work constructively together. In a facilitated workshop if the goal is not clear, a cohesive group will start to focus on a common enemy. Watch out – it may be
you, the facilitator!

The fundamental need for a common goal can also result in a cohesive
group blaming external parties for problems, rather than examining its
own deficiencies. This may affect the quality of the group's problem
solving processes. The facilitator therefore has to set a very clear
common goal for the group, and must remain focused on that goal
throughout the workshop.

STOP AND THINK!

Question 1

You're due to run a half-day workshop for an existing group of engineers. The discussion will be around the failure of a recent initiative to
improve productivity. The boss wants to be present, and you know he
has a domineering style. Can this workshop set-up work? If so, how? If
not, why not?

Question 2

A senior manager has asked you to run a one-day workshop to evaluate
the quality of the company newsletter, and to gather suggestions for
improvement. This workshop will bring together people from all over
the company with widely differing levels of responsibility and widely
differing jobs. Most of the people attending work out in the field on their
own, or in small satellite offices. The company culture is highly consultative, but this is normally done by e-mail. What are the potential advantages and disadvantages of this set-up? How would you maximize your
success?

CHAPTER 3

Planning a facilitated workshop

Speaking without thinking is like shooting without taking aim.
Old Spanish proverb

Workshop planning is essential. The plan should not be too detailed or too rigid, but a broad structure and purpose should be clearly thought out before the event. If the facilitator does not plan, the participants are likely to get a feeling of aimlessness about the workshop, or, worse still, one or two dominant members may hijack the event to address their own personal agendas.

Getting a clear purpose

A clear written purpose is fundamental for three main reasons. First, the facilitator needs to be sure of the purpose to enable him or her to design an effective event. Second, the participants need a clear purpose to hold them to prepare for the workshop. Third, other interested parties, such as a commissioning manager, must agree the purpose explicitly with the facilitator so that the right participants can be invited, and the right information is gathered.

The facilitator must fully understand the purpose of the workshop before committing to running the event. If the workshop theme comes from elsewhere it needs to be checked out thoroughly before you can go ahead with your planning. Even if the theme for the workshop is your own, you still need to make sure that you are clear abut how you would like people to contribute, and what you are hoping to come away with.

Often the facilitator does not 'own' the workshop. The workshop owner may be a manager in the organization who has specific ideas about what should be achieved. The facilitator should talk the workshop aims through with the relevant manager. This discussion should also cover who should attend, what they will be expected to contribute, how long the workshop should take, relevant research which could be done before the workshop takes place and what will happen to the workshop results when it's all over.

In some cases, the facilitator may simply be given a *fait accompli*, which he or she has to live with. Even in this scenario, the facilitator should still make a point of talking to the manager who commissioned the workshop to get a clear idea of what is required.

The workshop purpose should be written down in one or two sentences so that all participants can understand it. For example, a workshop aim which reads:

> This workshop is designed to address some client issues within the organization

is *not* clear enough for participants to prepare sensibly. It leaves open the questions of what issues; which clients; how should the issues be addressed. However, both of the workshop aims written below are clear and specific.

> This workshop focuses on the feedback received recently from our three major clients. We will examine the feedback and discuss what actions we need to take as a result.

> This workshop is to enable those present to give their views on the service provided by the in-house computer support team, with a view to improving this service.

The following checklist will help you to carry out a health check on your workshop aims. You should be able to answer yes to all of these questions.

- Is there a good reason for each participant to attend the workshop?
- Do you know what you are expecting each participant to contribute?
- Do you know what you want the participants to go away with?
- Do you know what will happen to the information generated by the workshop?

- Will the participants be making any firm decisions during the workshop, and if so, how will these decisions be made?
- Do you know what the expected outcomes are? (Decisions, preferences, a list of key issues, suggestions for solutions to a problem, creative ideas?)
- Are you well-informed about the subject matter under discussion? (If not, address this before the workshop.)
- Are the participants well-informed about the subject matter under discussion? (If not, this could be addressed before or during the workshop.)
- Do you have the right technical equipment (eg for demonstrations)?
- Do you know how to handle actions arising during the workshop?

Inviting participants

Once you have a clear workshop purpose, it should begin to be obvious whom to invite. Try to invite more than five people, but fewer than 12 as a guideline. This will mean you have enough people to create a lively discussion, but not so many that some voices go unheard.

Good reasons for inviting someone to attend are:

- the person has a lot of experience in the relevant area;
- you need the person's commitment;
- the person is an innovative thinker;
- the person is good at judging whether schemes will work;
- the person has good knowledge of relevant activities outside the organization;
- the person has good knowledge of relevant activities inside the organization;
- the person has influence;
- the person brings a fresh view on the problem.

Poor reasons for inviting someone to attend are:

- to make up the numbers;
- to ensure that a department is represented;
- because the person always comes;
- to avoid offence;
- to make the person feel involved, even though he or she has little to contribute.

Doing the right research

It is extremely unwise, and frankly unprofessional, to facilitate a workshop without any specific knowledge of the subject matter. You should research the topic as thoroughly as possible so that you can facilitate effectively, rather than simply act as nanny and scribe. You also need to ensure that participants have access to any relevant information either before the workshop begins or during the workshop.

A useful example of this is when a customer survey has been carried out and a workshop has been set up to discuss the results. In this case, you can give the participants the customer feedback to look at beforehand, or present it at the workshop, or invite the customer in question to attend the workshop and present his or her views face to face.

Another example is when non-technical employees are invited to contribute to a discussion of what the organization's future business requirements will be, with a view to creating new information technology solutions. Information about what can be achieved with the latest equipment might help these participants to contribute more constructively. This is normally done by one of the following methods:

- circulating written information beforehand;
- inviting suppliers to demonstrate their products;
- organizing a visit to other users to see some equipment in action.

You need to consider what relevant data might help the workshop's progress. This might include surveys or studies performed recently. You might be able to let participants see what other companies do in this area. The facilitator should have any available data ready at his or her fingertips to offer to workshop participants.

STOP AND THINK!

Question 1
Which of the three workshop aims below do you believe to be adequately clear?

- This workshop is to clarify our strategic thoughts.
- We are running a workshop to try to evaluate our appraisal scheme, with a view to making it better.

- We have a working account system, which we have decided to upgrade. This workshop is to generate requirements for the new accounting system.

Question 2

The Sales Manager of Fizzy Drinks Ltd wants to run a workshop to look at ideas for gaining more sales locally and within Europe. He wants to invite mainly shop floor staff and specifically wants to exclude managers, as he thinks they are out of touch. Is this a reasonable strategy?

Question 3

You have been asked to facilitate a workshop for a water company, which aims to gather requirements for a computer system to record and manage departmental performance information. You have very little knowledge of either the water industry or management information systems. How do you respond?

Designing the workshop

Now that you have a clear purpose, you know who is coming, and you have tackled the research issue, you can settle down to design the workshop. The workshop design is vital to the success of the workshop. It is your plan for how and in what order the issues will be captured and tackled. You must take time to design the workshop, and then to summarize the design in agenda form for circulation to all participants approximately one week before the workshop (participants do not need all the detail contained in a design).

How structured should the workshop be?

A facilitated workshop does not need to be planned as closely as a training session, but it cannot be as open and free ranging as an impromptu discussion. In a training session you are trying to help people learn something specific, so you have prescribed areas to cover. In a facilitated workshop, you are creating the right environment, atmosphere and opportunity for people to contribute in a constructive and positive way. You will need to home in on what is important to the

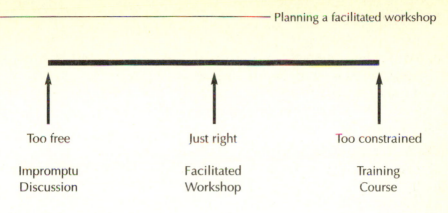

Figure 3.1   *Workshop structure scale*

participants, as well as cover prescribed territory. This means having a broad structure, without being too specific. A useful scale is represented in Figure 3.1.

It is tempting to miss out the planning, and to hope that a process of questioning and listening, and allowing the participants to dictate their own agenda will be good enough. However, this method has its drawbacks:

- the discussion may wander off the prescribed topic, or become repetitive if there is a lack of structure;
- the participants may get restless, and feel that the workshop isn't going anywhere;
- interest may not be maintained if there is not enough variety in the workshop;
- key issues may not be given enough time.

On the other hand, if the facilitator is too prescriptive with a rigorous list of prepared questions, the drawbacks are:

- the pace may be too fast and furious for any real discussion to emerge;
- participants become frustrated as they are dragged through a list of prepared questions, unable to bring up other issues;
- there is no option to skip irrelevant or overlapping questions;
- unforeseen important topics may be missed.

The ideal structure lies somewhere between the two. It will probably consist of a few carefully chosen opening questions, some set tasks and the use of specific discussion tools to elicit and record contributions (see descriptions of various discussion tools in the following sections). Extra questions should be held 'on the back burner' in case the first few do not open up enough discussion.

Basic design rules

There are some basic rules that need to be absorbed before you design a workshop. These rules will help you to maximize the contribution from each participant.

- *People feel comfortable when they know what is coming next* – so do not keep them in the dark. Set out a clear structure and keep to it, even if you negotiate changes to elements of the structure. If you make any big changes to the timetable, then let the participants know – so do not flog a room full of dead horses. When you are the facilitator you are on show, and therefore have extra energy and stamina. This is created by an increase in the adrenaline level in your body. The participants do not have this level of stimulation, so you need to plan in regular breaks or changes of activity to allow people to move around, stretch or change position.
- *People have basic human needs that interface with their concentration* – so remember to plan in coffee breaks, lunch and loo breaks. Alternatively you can just let people help themselves at any time to refreshments, or pop out to the loo whenever they need to. You do need to tell participants if you're expecting them to follow the latter plan, otherwise they will tend to assume that they need to wait for breaks. This can have uncomfortable consequences!
- *People will concentrate for longer if the activity is altered slightly every 15 to 30 minutes* – changes of activity help people to refresh their concentration. This may involve changing the physical activity, or changing the area of mental focus.
- *Start with the simple, and move to the complex* – lead people into complex issues step by step. It is more helpful if you have everyone up to speed on an issue, rather than just the one or two participants with very agile minds.
- *Start with the simple, then break it down into parts* – our brains work well if we understand both the big picture and its constituent parts. It is particularly helpful if we can relate the two views. For example, a workshop on organizational communication problems could start by

asking participants to finish the two sentences 'Communication in this organization is…' and 'Communication in this organization should be…' This addresses the big picture. The next step would be to look at the different elements of organizational communication such as company meetings, senior management meetings, inter-departmental communication, e-mail, memos, telephones, coffee room chat, gossip, etc.

● *Start with the safe and move to the risky* – if, for example, your team has been heavily criticized, don't start with the criticisms immediately. Do some warming up on some safe issues, such as the team's strengths, to get everyone relaxed.

● *People will be swayed by majority voting and the views of the most dominant members of the group when asked to commit in public to a point of view* – the story is very different if anonymous views are sought. Although managers and staff members insist that this is not the case, the author's experience and the evidence of published research indicate that this is true. See Chapter 2 for further information. This effect should be taken very seriously, and must be overcome by skilled use of anonymous voting techniques, discussed later in this section.

Typical workshop sequence

Every workshop follows a basic sequence of steps as follows:

Step 1 Welcome and introduction

The facilitator welcomes the group, ensures that everyone knows who everyone else is and relaxes everyone, possibly via a short introductory exercise (see later in this chapter for some examples of introductory exercises). The workshop aims are made clear and participants get a chance to question these aims. The workshop structure is set up, and the workshop ground rules agreed.

Step 2 Topic focus

The facilitator begins with a question or activity that allows the participants to focus on the workshop topic at the top level. For example, a workshop addressing a specific problem could start by giving everyone a chance to write down how he or she has been affected by the problem. This allows everyone to clear out the worries of the day, and focus on the workshop.

Steps 3, 4, 5 Specific topic sessions

Specific topic sessions should be used to address the relevant topic from various angles, discussing different pieces of information, or discussing different areas of the subject. For instance, a workshop that aims to make improvements to the way projects are managed might be split into specific topics such as:

● managing the task;
● managing the team;
● managing the client.

Step 6 Recap of conclusions and decision making

The conclusions reached in the specific topic sessions should be revisited, and possibly opened up for comment. Overall conclusions and decisions can then be recorded.

Step 7 Wrap up and next steps

The facilitator should call the workshop to a close by thanking everyone for his or her contributions and explaining very clearly what will happen next, when it will happen and who will be responsible.

Varying workshop activity

Within the broad structure above, you will need to plan a range of activities. You can use a big group question and answer format throughout, but you will find this less effective than a more varied and stimulating programme. I am not advocating a mad, action-packed bonanza. You need to be quite clear on the difference between appropriate stimulation and gimmicks.

Some simple techniques can be used to vary the activity in a workshop. Some possibilities are:

● brainstorming ideas as a large group;
● splitting into groups;
● asking small groups to present the fruit of their discussion on particular issues;
● asking people to think about their own experiences, both positive and negative;
● using quotes to start discussions (eg 'There is no such thing as society' for a workshop on the organization's role in the local community);

- looking at the pros and cons of different options;
- using yellow stickers to elicit input;
- asking participants to finish a phrase (eg 'This department's key strength is...');
- ranking options written on cards;
- using a quiz to get people thinking;
- using case studies to get discussion about key issues;
- voting for different options.

See the next section for detailed descriptions of tools and techniques.

Workshop tools and techniques

There are several tried and tested tools that can be used to vary the activity in a workshop, maintain interest and involvement, encourage creativity and provide structure to the discussion. These techniques can be divided into four broad groups, which are discussed below.

Introduction techniques

The workshop introduction is crucial because it sets the tone for the whole of the session. Participants will be scrutinizing your competence as facilitator, and will tend to follow the mood you set. This means that your introduction has to be bright, purposeful and stimulating. It also needs to get the participants into a frame of mind where they are keen to contribute.

The introduction techniques below are designed to allow participants to begin to focus on the topic in question, relax, get comfortable and get to know each other (if necessary). You may also wish to have some information about who is who, and what their expectations are. The introduction also provides the useful function of getting everyone to speak. If this does not happen, some of the more reticent individuals never get over that hurdle of uttering their first contribution.

Avoid diving headlong into the business of the workshop without giving participants a chance to feel comfortable. Also avoid the trap that many workshops fall into of indulging in long irrelevant personal inductions. Getting each participant to 'say a little about himself or herself' may get rather tedious for the participants, especially if 'a little' turns out to be a lot. Make the introductions snappy and to the point, and make a point of asking each participant one follow-up question as you go around the group. This gets participants into an interactive mode, and let them know that you're listening.

Try to be inventive with your introductions. The following list might give you some ideas.

- Please give me your name, your role and two things you like about the computer services centre.
- Tell me who you are and give me two things that you enjoy about working for this organization.
- Introduce the person on your left and say why you think he or she is here (you may have to give them five minutes to familarize themselves with each other).
- Which functional character most closely describes your role at this workshop today?
- Tell me who you are and how you would like to be feeling at the end of the workshop.
- Tell me who you are and why you are here, using the structure 'My name is... and I'm here to...'
- Use an adjective beginning with the same letter as your name to describe your current attitude to this project. For example Disinterested Derek, Optimistic Oliver or Irritated Irene.

Discussion openers

Discussion openers are designed to get participants to open up their ideas on the topic in question by considering the subject at the top level. Openers should not encourage any detailed exchange of information; they should only solicit broad views.

Yellow stickers

Ask participants to finish a phrase three different ways using three yellow stickers. For example, the phrase could be 'I believe that the three most important features of this product are...'. Participants then stick the completed stickers up on a large flipchart and the facilitator reads them out for the whole group. The participants can then chip in with further explanations. The ideas gathered may then be used as a basis for further discussion, or they can stay as they are, simply representing top-level views on the subject. They should be referred back to from time to time during the workshop.

Individual notes

Ask each individual to spend five minutes reflecting on his or her own experiences or interests. This five minutes could be spent for instance listing three good (or bad) experiences of a particular product or service, or three key issues of personal importance on the topic under discussion.

When the five minutes is up, the facilitator writes at least one idea from each person up on the flipchart. This can be used as a basis for further discussion, or as a reference point to link back to later in the workshop.

Making a list in twos

Ask individuals to pair up with a neighbour and work on producing something together. This could be a list of the good and bad features of an internal service department, or a long list of all the issues they wish to air during the workshop. When the list is complete, the facilitator should write at least one idea from each couple up on the flipchart. This can then be used as a basis for further discussion, or as a reference point to link back to later in the workshop.

Filling in a questionnaire

Questionnaires can provide a good initial focus for a workshop. The questionnaire in Chapter 1 is a good example of a discussion-provoking questionnaire. You could create a simple, relevant ten-question questionnaire, allowing the participant to select one response from: True, False or Don't Know. Hand it out, ask people to fill it in anonymously and then collate the answers. A neat way of collating responses is to shuffle the questionnaires, hand them back out to the participants, and then ask for a show of hands on each question. This way you can quickly note down the number of 'True' responses for each question without losing anonymity. Figure 3.2 shows a sample questionnaire that was used to open a computer services review workshop.

Note that anonymous responses are generally more honest than responses made openly in front of the group. See Chapter 2 for reasons for this. Responses from questionnaires provide a good starting point for discussion, as they tend to reveal views that normally go unheard. The data collated via a questionnaire provides a good numerical record of the views of those present at the workshop.

No.	Question	Tick if TRUE	Tick if FALSE	Tick if you DON'T KNOW
1	The telephones are answered promptly			
2	The technical advice given is useful			
3	I always get enough information about the progress of my call			
4	The service is courteous			
5	My urgent problems are always fixed quickly			
6	Fixes usually work first time			
7	When new software is installed, I am made aware of how to use it			
8	My ideas for long-term improvements are taken seriously			
9	The service gets better and better			
10	I am generally satisfied with the service			

Figure 3.2 *Opening questionnaire*

Structured discussion tools

Structured discussion tools are very useful for directing discussion, encouraging contributions and recording views.

Brainstorming

This well-known technique is good for generating a list of ideas for further discussion. Brainstorming works best with a group of at least five people. The people need to be quite relaxed and comfortable. You need a flipchart and a pen.

The facilitator must begin by clearly setting out the subject for the brainstorm, and explaining that this part of the workshop is about *generating* ideas, not *evaluating* them – so all ideas are acceptable. The rules of the brainstorm should be communicated to the group.

- Each person takes a turn to come up with an idea, starting at the first person and working round.
- The idea is written up on the flipchart verbatim by the facilitator, without evaluation, categorization or clarification by anyone.
- If any person does not have an idea, he or she says 'pass'.
- Fifteen minutes is spent collating ideas this way.
- When most people are saying 'pass' the facilitator opens up for final ideas and then closes the brainstorm.
- The facilitator moves on to open the discussion of the ideas generated.

All the way through the brainstorm, the facilitator encourages the group to come up with more ideas, build on existing ideas or branch out from what has already been said. When the brainstorm is finished, the facilitator can then go back through each item, getting people to discuss it in more detail. This discussion process is very important, and on no account should be left out.

The facilitator should avoid the standard brainstorm pitfalls.

- Evaluating the ideas as they come; this serves only to block the flow of ideas.
- Writing too much per contribution; this blocks the flow of ideas too.
- Categorizing the ideas ('Oh we've had something like that already...'); again this blocks the flow.
- Closing down the brainstorm too soon rather than pushing for ideas ('Well that's about it, I guess...').
- Using brainstorming to generate ideas which are entirely obvious and require little thought or creativity.

The brainstorming technique will work for topics such as:

- generating ideas for improving a product;
- getting ideas for new products or services;
- listing all the possible courses of action.

The example brainstorm in Figure 3.3 was produced by a team of service engineers for an electrical repair company. This list was then whittled down to the most useful suggestions, which led to some innovative improvements in the service.

How to make our service better

Cheaper
Smile more
Get there quicker
Offer extras
Carry more spares
More flexible with times
Mobile phones
Look professional
Ask them what they want
Feedback forms
Clear up
Air freshener
Bring a bunch of flowers
Give a free electrical survey
Offer to look at other things
Trade in service for duff equipment
Price catalogues
Pay by credit card
Fridge overhauls

Figure 3.3 *Example of a brainstormed list*

The example brainstorm in Figure 3.3 was produced by a team of service engineers for an electrical repair company. This list was then whittled down to the most useful suggestions, which led to some innovative improvements in the service.

Spider brainstorming

Spider brainstorming is a version of the list-generating brainstorm described above. Rather than generating a serial list of ideas, the spider brainstorm creates a spider diagram of connected ideas. This can be useful for untangling complex topics and provides a good visual tool for group discussion.

Use spider brainstorming to capture all the ideas relating to a particular theme. You need a group of at least five, a whiteboard and a pen. A whiteboard is better than a flipchart because you may need to reposition items as you go along.

First agree the theme or subject, and write this in an oval at the centre of the board. Brainstorm related issues and subjects. Spread these around the board.

If items are linked then draw lines between them. Select three or four key categories and draw a rectangle around each. Connect each remaining idea with a line to a specific category. You may need to redraw the map. Use the resulting information to guide discussion.

The spider brainstorming technique will work for topics such as:

- looking at the cause of a problem;
- generating business or system requirements;
- deciding on the contents of a document.

An example spider brainstorm appears in Figure 3.4.

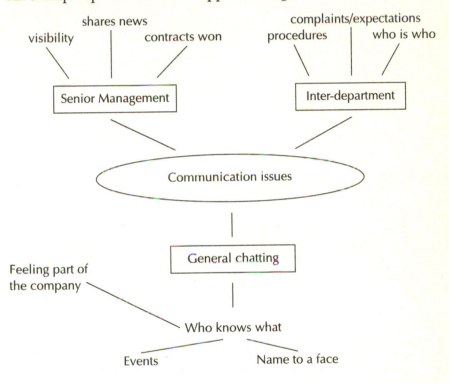

Figure 3.4 *Example of spider brainstorm*

Techniques for whittling down the ideas

When you generate a large number of ideas in a workshop, you usually need to whittle those ideas down to the best few. This should be done by first discussing each idea in an open forum to gain a full understanding of what is meant. The facilitator plays an important role here in pressing for clarity and logic. When all ideas are understood, one of the following techniques can be used for whittling the ideas down.

- *Show of hands* – ask each individual to vote for the five most favoured ideas via a show of hands as you run through the ideas.
- *Flipchart ticking* – participants are asked to use a flipchart pen to tick their five most favoured items directly on the flipchart/whiteboard. Do this informally over coffee, so that participants' votes are not scrutinized by their colleagues.
- *Gold stars and red spots* – participants are given five gold stars and five red spots. They are asked to stick one gold star against each most favoured option on the flipchart, and one red spot against each least favoured option. Again, do this informally.
- *Individual allocation of points* – each participant allocates a number of points (for example ten points) across their five most favoured options, writing these directly on the flipchart. Again, do this informally.

Any of the above can be done using individual copies of the list of ideas. These can be collated using the secret voting technique below.

Balance sheets

A balance sheet can be used to evaluate and compare various courses of action. This technique works well for examining various solutions to a complex problem.

The course of action under discussion (eg hire a temporary receptionist next week), should be clearly written at the top of a flipchart sheet so that everyone can see it. A line is then drawn down the middle of the flipchart. The facilitator asks participants for the advantages of the option. These advantages are written to the left of the line. Arrows are usually drawn as on Figure 3.5. A grading scale for importance can also be used (eg marks out of five). The disadvantages are dealt with identically, but to the right of the line.

Figure 3.5 shows a balance sheet that was drawn up by a group of managers facing a crisis in their sales office. They were discussing various courses of action, and this was option number 3. Pros are listed on the left and cons on the right. Scores out of five have been agreed by the participants to indicate the relative importance of each item.

Once you have considered a number of options in this way, you can select the best option by simply comparing the overall scores, or you can carry out a final vote where each participant selects his or her most favoured option.

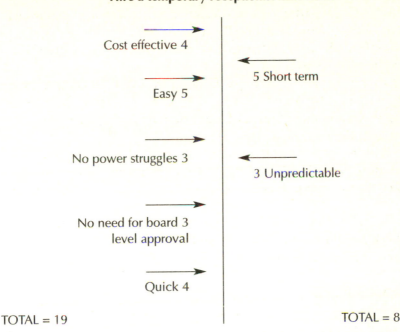

Option 3
Hire a temporary receptionist next week

Cost effective 4

5 Short term

Easy 5

No power struggles 3

3 Unpredictable

No need for board 3
level approval

Quick 4

TOTAL = 19   TOTAL = 8

Figure 3.5 *Example balance sheet*

Small group work

A good way of varying activity in a workshop is to split large groups up into small groups to carry out particular tasks. Small group work encourages participants to discuss and reflect on issues, rather than to state opinions. It also keeps interest levels up and allows the more reticent members of the group to contribute in a less formal, more intimate forum. Small groups should comprise two to five people. Groups larger than five need to be facilitated. Left alone they may lose focus. The principles of running small group tasks are:

● set very specific and clear tasks;
● give the groups an end time for the task, and be reasonably strict with this;
● check progress according to time, and if they must run over, negotiate a small increase with all the groups;

- ask each group to bring something back to the large group (an idea, a conclusion, a list);
- go round to check that each group understands what it is supposed to be doing.

Examples of small group activities are:

- list all the possible solutions to a particular problem, and select your favoured five;
- discuss and categorize a list of the pros and cons of a particular action;
- generate a list of current problems with a particular service or product.

Mini presentations

Mini presentations follow on from small group work. This method encourages involvement and generates interest. Ask each small group working on a group task to formally present their key findings. Encourage the groups to select their presenter early on, and follow the rules below:

- give participants a set time for the presentation (five or ten minutes) and be strict on this;
- ask each presenter to use one or two clear flipchart sheets to illustrate what is being said;
- formally invite the other groups to comment on or criticize what has been said.

Decision making: open voting and secret voting

In a facilitated workshop you can make group decisions in one of two basic ways: open voting or secret voting.

Open voting involves having the usual show of hands either to indicate a preference by allocating scores to options, or to indicate a 'yes' or 'no' to a particular option. In workshops where decisions must be made, facilitators often use a majority-voting scheme where a decision is passed as long as 80 per cent of the participants are in agreement. The 'silence is compliance' rule sometimes used in rapid software development workshops is fallible because people will not necessarily speak out publicly against the majority.

A *secret vote* is a way of getting people's views without the stronger, more powerful members of the group influencing the others. For example, participants are asked to allocate 20 points across their five most favoured options, giving more points to the options that they prefer. Each participant records his or her votes anonymously on a piece of paper.

At this point, the facilitator could add up all the scores while the participants twiddle their thumbs. However, involvement and interest can be maintained by getting the group to help with the scoring. Shuffle and redistribute the papers. Now each participant has an anonymous set of votes. The facilitator then goes through each option, asking for points allocated for each option one at a time. The scores will then be displayed on a flipchart.

This technique could also be used to select the five most important ideas resulting from a brainstorming session, or to decide the relative weight of various pros and cons collected in a balance sheet.

Fuzzy discussion tools

The structured discussion tools described in the previous section are ideal for discussions that centre on reasonably well-prescribed ideas. However, sometimes workshops have to address issues which are more difficult to pin down, such as:

- company vision;
- company culture;
- management style;
- inter-departmental difficulties.

For these types of issues, although some structured discussion tools will help, a less rigorous approach may be necessary. The tools listed below will help to address fuzzy issues.

Mad, sad, glad table

A useful technique is the mad, sad or glad table. Ask participants what makes them mad, sad or glad about the issues in question. If you are discussing company vision, workshop participants can split into small groups to list what things made them mad, sad or glad about the organization. The headings mad, sad and glad are intentionally vague, to enable people to discuss the fuzzy issues without having to be precise. The precision will come later. An example list from a small group discussing management style in a medium sized engineering company in the UK appears in Figure 3.6.

As facilitator, you can then gather the data together and get the group to discuss the relative importance of each item. The really important issues can then be tackled in more detail.

MAD	SAD	GLAD
No reports come out of management meetings. We want to know what is going on inside the company	Communication between staff and managers was better before the office move	The company get-togethers are very good. Thank you!
Senior management never come and speak to us	I never want to be a manager because I know how much they are disliked	The newsletter gives clear information on contracts won
They get paid too much!		Managers are open to suggestions
The management offices have better carpets than ours		We enjoy our jobs

Figure 3.6 *Mad, sad, glad table*

Futuring

Futuring is especially useful for company visiting workshops. It is a creative technique which gets participants to think about what they want for the future. An example is 'Imagine you are sitting in a workshop five years from now. How would you like the organization to be and what would you like to be discussing?' This could equally be used to discuss management style. For example 'You are about to attend a management meeting three years from now. Describe the meeting format and management style you would like to be in place three years from now.'

Open space

Part of the workshop can be labelled an open space. This means that there is no agenda for that portion of time. The purpose is to get participants to discuss 'burning issues' which they select themselves. The facilitator organizes everyone to sit in a circle, with a space in the centre. Pens and paper lie on the floor in the centre of the space, and participants are invited to write down a burning issue for all to see, thus committing to running a short discussion group based around that issue.

Once a satisfactory number of burning issues have been written down, the group divides according to choice, and short mini-workshops are held. The small groups come back with a summary of their main points.

One of the interesting principles of open space is that participants are given permission to flit from group to group, stay put or say nothing. This makes the atmosphere very free, and has liberating effects on participants.

Acting out

The process of acting out particular scenes from organizational life is a good way of raising difficult or complex issues without getting people to actually vocalize those issues. For instance, a small group of participants attending a workshop addressing company culture could be asked to act out two scenes. The first might be a scene that represents company culture as it is now. The second might be a scene that represents company culture as it should be, or could be.

You can be even more creative by asking participants to use a favourite TV programme format such as *The News*, or a quiz show, or any children's programme such as *Blue Peter* or *Sesame Street* to get across their frustrations with company culture. This can be very enjoyable and memorable for participants, while still addressing serious issues.

When the scenes are over, you can ask the group to come up with key points arising from the scenes acted out in front of the group.

River of life

If you are facilitating a workshop which is addressing an issue behind which there is a lot of important history, you can ask participants to discuss and untangle the relevant history by using the 'River of life' technique. This involves splitting the participants into small groups and asking them to produce a group drawing of a river on a large blank page (a flipchart page is best). This river should represent the history of the organization, or department or product. The river can have bends, waterfalls, dams, weirs, bridges, splits or it can even dry up altogether. Ask the participants to label every significant point in the river's path. This enables the group to raise and discuss any complex or difficult issues.

Bring the groups together and ask them to present their pictures to each other. After the ensuing discussion, the facilitator should help the group to identify the most important moments in the history of the relevant organization, department or product. This should help to take the discussion on to talk about the present and the future.

The key advantage of this technique is that it allows participants to get worrying or concerning issues from the past out of the way before talking about the future.

Collage

Collage is a good small group activity, which can be used to get participants to discuss any difficult or complex issues. Give the participants a stack of magazines with a variety of types of picture, scissors, an A3 sheet of paper and some glue. They can then create a collage which represents management style or company culture either as it is now, or how they would like it to be. The groups explain their collages to each other, and any key issues are collected by the facilitator for further discussion.

Putting it all together

Once you have a clear workshop aim, you know who to invite, you've done the necessary research, and you have some familiarity with the relevant tools and techniques, you can then begin to place a structure around the step sequence referred to above. A generic structure appears below.

Step 1 Welcome and introduction

Welcome everyone, and introduce the workshop topic and aims. Talk through the workshop agenda, and set out any important workshop ground rules. Use one of the introduction techniques listed above to get everyone comfortable, and to focus on the topic area. Remember to include everyone.

Step 2 Topic focus

Use one of the discussion openers listed above to open up the topic. Get discussion going round the issues raised.

Steps 3, 4, 5 Specific topic sessions

Home in on specific areas and use the structured discussion tools described above to make your way through the necessary creation of ideas, general discussion and decision making. A typical sequence is:

- brainstorm to generate ideas;
- discussion of ideas;
- whittle ideas down using secret voting or flipchart ticking;
- group work on pros and cons;
- mini presentations of group findings;
- group discussion;
- final decision using open or secret voting.

Step 6 Recap of conclusions

Recap on all decisions made, lists generated and options selected. Overall conclusions can then be recorded.

Step 7 Wrap up and next steps

Call the workshop to a close by running through what you think was said, what was felt and what was decided. This gives an opportunity for last minute additions or corrections. Be clear about what information will be sent to whom, and what will be done by when.

An example workshop design appears below. Note that the design is mainly for the facilitator's use, to plan the session. The participants should receive an agenda (see next section) which will help them to do some pre-thinking before the workshop begins.

In-House Computer Support Workshop Design

	Time and activity	Duration	Who
9.00	Welcome and introduction	15 mins	Full group
9.15	Presentation and discussion of last year's survey results	15 mins	Full group

	Reflect on individual experiences this year	15 mins	Individual
9.45	Discussion of individual experiences, pulling out good points and bad points	20 mins	Small groups
	Full group discussion Using secret voting to rank good points in order of importance and bad points according to importance/urgency	40 mins	Full group
10.45	COFFEE		
11.00	The ideal service? – brainstorm ideas	20 mins	Full group
	Discuss, evaluate and give priorities using show of hands	20 mins	Full group
11.40	Three things we want from the support service in the future (over the next five years)	20 mins	Small groups
	Mini presentation from small groups	30 mins	Full group
12.30	Wrap up	15 mins	Full group
12.45	CLOSE		

STOP AND THINK!

Question 4

A management consultancy employs 15 staff, ten of whom are management consultants. These people normally work out in the field with clients, and rarely meet as one big group. The workshop design below aims to allow the group of ten management consultants to discuss and decide on a business strategy for the next five years. Would it work? Give your reasons.

Business Strategy Workshop Design

	Time and activity	Duration	Who
9.00	Welcome and introduction Our views and our personal aims	30 mins	Full group
9.30	List individual ideas for new strategic directions	10 mins	Individual
	Full group discussion of new strategic directions Whittle down to the favoured few	20 mins	Full group
10.00	Small group discussion of potential gains and resources needed for each option Small groups prepare mini-presentation of findings	90 mins	Small groups
11.30	COFFEE		
11.50	Full group discussion of options, using balance sheets and secret voting to decide on most favoured options	40 mins	Full group
12.30	Wrap up	15 mins	Full group
12.45	CLOSE		

Question 5

A group of 15 recruitment agency staff currently work from an office in the centre of town. The company is considering closing the office, and getting staff to work from home. Design a workshop which allows the staff to give their views on home-working, and lets them give their thoughts on what facilities and processes would need to be in place to make this option work. Use the template below.

Workshop template

_____ **Workshop Design**

Time and activity	Duration	Who

Producing an agenda

The agenda goes out to participants, and is an important part of the whole workshop process. It lets people know what the workshop is about, and gives them some ideas on how they can prepare for the workshop. It is not useful to give participants the workshop design, as it contains too much information. Below is an example agenda, which could be used to inform participants about the workshop designed in the previous section.

Example workshop agenda

In-House Computer Support Workshop

Thursday 20th November

Agenda

You have been selected to attend the above workshop because we wish to get your ideas and views about the in-house computer support service. The purpose of this workshop is to gain a clearer picture of what is good about the service, what improvements are needed and what will be required from the service in the future.
Please have a think about the topics below before you come.

9.00	Welcome and introduction
	Presentation of last year's survey results
	Discussion of participants' experiences of the service during this year – good and bad
10.45	COFFEE
11.00	What would the ideal service be?
11.40	Participants' requirements for the future service – next five years
12.30	Wrap up
12.45	CLOSE

STOP AND THINK!

Question 6

What are the strengths and weaknesses of the following workshop agenda? *We are meeting on Wednesday morning to discuss leadership in this organization. It has been noted that leadership is lacking in some parts of the company and we wish to rectify this. Please come with some clear ideas on how this state of affairs can be improved.*

CHAPTER 4

Running a facilitated workshop

Every crowd has a silver lining
PT Barnum

The facilitator's job is to get the very best out of the assembled group. No matter how unpromising the group looks, or how tedious the subject matter, a facilitator who follows the guidelines set out in this section can get any group of people talking, thinking and contributing positively.

The facilitator's responsibility on the day

The facilitator is responsible for ensuring that the workshop runs smoothly from start to finish. This means keeping an eye on the participants, the aims and the physical aspects of the workshop. The facilitator needs to guide the participants through the workshop by:

● welcoming everyone to the workshop both as they enter the room and at the start of the programme for the day;
● introducing participants to each other if necessary;
● making sure that participants are safe, comfortable, fed and watered;
● creating a relaxed, participative atmosphere;
● watching participants to make sure that they are involved;
● dealing with participants who are being awkward;
● encouraging participants to build on ideas and to think in new ways;
● staying afterwards to chat to participants about any concerns.

The facilitator also needs to make sure that the workshop aims are clear, and that the necessary work is done by:

- making the aims, structure and timetable explicit;
- being very clear about what is expected;
- guiding the group through the pre-prepared tasks and questions;
- questioning participants about their views to ensure that the whole group understands the points being made;
- checking that participants are clear about what is being said, or about what they are being asked to do;
- keeping the discussion focused;
- bringing relevant information to the attention of the participants;
- moving the discussion on when necessary;
- covering the ground;
- making sure that workshop timing is managed;
- keeping a record of the discussion (flipchart or notes);
- extracting actions and decisions where necessary.

The physical set-up is also important. The facilitator is responsible for:

- checking the equipment beforehand (Do the pens work? Has the flipchart got paper on it?);
- ensuring that the room is set-up so that everyone can see the flipchart/whiteboard;
- clearing away any confidential information from the work area after the workshop has finished.

STOP AND THINK!

Question 1

Imagine you are facilitating a workshop for ten managers. You are expecting a flipchart to be present but there is only an overhead projector. What would you do?

Question 2

A participant arrives at the workshop, warmly shakes your hand and announces that he is only observing for interest, so he will sit at the back. Is this OK by you?

Introducing the workshop

Time should be set aside at the start of the workshop to perform a clear introduction. The group should also be put at their ease, and be quite clear about what the workshop is about.

The tone of the workshop is set in the introduction, so it's important to get it right. Use the checklist below to make sure that nothing is missed:

- welcome everyone and thank them for coming;
- introduce yourself, and explain your role;
- explain the workshop purpose and background (if the workshop has been organized or sponsored by a senior individual, get him or her to introduce the workshop purpose; this will let the participants know that the workshop is important);
- describe the wider process, of which this workshop is a part;
- describe the structure and timing of the session, indicating when breaks are and explaining where to get coffee or lunch;
- tell people where the loos are! (This seems obvious, but it is very important and often forgotten);
- cover fire/safety arrangements (what to do in the event of a fire);
- explain the style of the workshop, and set any ground rules (see section on Managing the discussion later in this chapter);
- decide who is going to record what happens (the facilitator's flipchart may be enough);
- get the participants to introduce themselves (see Introduction techniques in Chapter 3).

Questioning and listening

The facilitator should be able to lead the group comfortably through a series of pre-planned topics and tasks using a combination of listening and questioning skills. Participants need to have the feeling that their views are being taken seriously, so you cannot merely follow a sequence of standard questions.

Listening skills

A lot of nonsense is talked about listening skills. Listening is not just about nodding and giving airtime; it is also about making sure you understand what the other person is saying. In a group situation, this is not normally done. People will compete for space to state their own opinions, but will rarely take the time to find out what is really meant by the previous speaker.

In a workshop, the facilitator cannot simply let participants shout out opinions. These opinions have to be based on fact, and the facts have to be challenged and explained. If a participant makes a statement, which is based on gut feeling, then that has to be explained, and some of the influences behind that gut feeling expanded upon.

The physical side of good listening is important. The facilitator should demonstrate good listening by:

- maintaining good eye contact with the speaker;
- nodding;
- facing the person;
- showing expression on his or her face;
- not fiddling;
- not looking at the clock!;
- avoiding face-touching gestures (see the section on Body language later in this chapter);
- confirming what was said by recording contributions on the flipchart (participants can get quite cross if their comments are not written up).

The spoken part of listening is even more important. It is about striving to understand another person's point of view. This means:

- expressing empathy (eg 'I see what you mean' or 'That sounds problematic' or 'That must have been a surprise');
- using good direct questions (see the next section in this chapter);
- using summaries to clarify what has been said ('So you're saying that the service has been only 80 per cent effective over the past 6 months');
- suspending judgement until the comment is properly explored;
- treating each person's perception as reality – never discounting a participant's view;
- never using sarcasm or ridicule;
- thanking participants for their input.

While the main topics for discussion are pre-planned, the follow-on questions have to be determined on the spot. This is an important part of making the workshop useful. Every person must leave the workshop feeling that he or she contributed something.

Questioning skills and question types

Questioning skills are very important throughout the workshop, but are particularly useful for large group discussion. Large group discussion has to be controlled, without being stilted.

Useful questions to ask can be broadly categorized into six types:

Open questions

Open questions are used to open up discussion and get people thinking. An open question cannot be answered with a simple 'Yes' or 'No' response. Questions such as 'What are the main responsibilities of this department?' and 'Which aspects of this organization are attractive to you?' are good discussion openers.

Most of the key open questions would probably be pre-prepared by the facilitator before the workshop takes place, but it is useful to be able to use them if you have to move into unplanned areas of discussion.

Be careful not to be too facile or too vague. A question such as 'What do you think about the system?' is likely to elicit far less response than 'What parts of the system are you unhappy with?' People do not respond to questions that are either too obvious or too obscure. In addition 'Tell me about one good experience you have had of using this service' works better than 'Tell me about this product'. The latter is too vague.

Clarifying questions

Clarifying questions provide the facilitator with a very useful tool. A clarifying question asks for further information to clarify a point. For example, the facilitator in the workshop conversation reproduced below is using clarifying questions to understand a participant's point of view. This example illustrates how clarification can lead to a better quality discussion:

Participant: 'I think the systems staff have become lazy and complacent.'
Facilitator: 'What makes you say that?'
Participant: 'They never answer the phone, and when they do it's to tell you that you should be able to fix your own problems.'

Facilitator: 'I see. That sounds bad. How often does this happen?'

Participant: 'Well, last week it took me six attempts at ringing them before I could get someone to pick up the phone. It just rings and rings.'

Facilitator: 'OK. I'm writing the phone issue on the flipchart because it sounds pretty serious. What about this business of not addressing problems. How serious is that?'

Participant: 'Well, I suppose they do address problems. It was just that after calling six times, I was so mad that when the guy had the cheek to tell me I should ask my local secretary to replace the printer cartridge, it really got my goat!'

Facilitator: 'Yes, I can understand that. Bad timing. But do you still want to raise this issue about not addressing problems?'

Participant: 'No, no. That was a one-off really. Just stick to the initial problem of not answering the phone.'

Example questions

Example questions are used in the same way as clarifying questions: to give further insight. An example question asks for an instance of a particular issue, and is illustrated in the conversation below:

Participant: 'This organization is actually rather good at keeping in touch with the customer view of our services. Their views can lead directly to service improvements.'

Facilitator: 'Good. That sounds very positive. Can you give a recent example of a customer view that led to a service improvement?'

Probe questions

A probe question burrows down into a topic to get specific information. This converges the discussion into particular areas, for example 'What was particularly impressive about her telephone manner?'

Too many probe questions will come across as aggressive, so be wary of overdoing it with this type of question. Cushioning language can be used to soften a probe question. The example below shows how a cushioned probe question can reveal more information than a straightforward probe.

Straightforward probe:

Participant: 'Well, I just told the guy to clear his desk and leave.'

Facilitator: 'Why did you do that?'

Participant: 'It's obvious. He was useless!'

Cushioned probe:
Participant: 'Well, I just told the guy to clear his desk and leave.'
Facilitator: 'Can you say on reflection what made you act that way?'
Participant: 'Well, John over there will back me up. We gave him every chance to pull his socks up, but he never really seemed to want to try.'

Reflective questions:

It can be useful for the facilitator to simply reflect back the mood of the participant, to glean more information:

Participant: 'So the customer says we don't seem to care?'
Facilitator: 'That's what the survey says. You seem confused by that.'
Participant: 'Yes. The feedback from the customers I spoke to recently was quite the opposite.'

Particular words used by the participant can also be reflected back to elicit more information, for example:

Participant: 'I find that statement quite worrying.'
Facilitator: 'Worrying?'
Participant: 'Yes. I thought these issues had been solved.'

Encouragements

An encouraging enquiry can be used to get more information from participants. Such enquiries include questions addressed to the whole group, such as:

- 'Are there any more views on that topic?'
- 'Has anyone else got anything pressing they want to say?'
- 'Does anyone want to add to this list?'
- 'Has anyone got any strong feelings about what has been said already?'
- 'Any other comments?'

or questions addressed to individuals:

- 'Go on...'
- 'That sounds interesting. Can you tell us more?'

STOP AND THINK!

Question 3

Ask a clarifying question in reply to the following participant contribution: 'I have always found this company to be mean-minded and mealy-mouthed'.

Question 4

Ask a cushioned probe question in response to the following participant contribution: 'There's no way we can use any of this utter rubbish your guys have developed!'

Managing the discussion

The facilitator's most important job on the day is to manage the workshop discussion. He or she must make sure that the discussion is free enough to allow varied, creative contributions, but controlled enough to ensure that the whole group is involved, and that the necessary ground is covered in the time available.

A well-prepared workshop design is fundamental to good workshop management. The facilitator needs to steer participants through the design while giving them enough freedom to think about the topic, discuss ideas and come to any necessary conclusions.

Agreeing ground rules

Ground rules provide a good basis for discussion management. The facilitator can either use a typical set as a starting point or ask the participants to co-create a list from scratch. A typical set of ground rules would be:

- listen to each other;
- strive to understand other people's views;
- don't talk over each other;
- share airtime equally;
- say if you don't understand;
- say if you don't agree;
- be honest;

- suspend judgement until you understand;
- be prepared to discuss the reasons for your views.

It is time consuming to get the group to create their own ground rules. This approach would only be appropriate for a longer workshop of at least two days. However, if participants are involved in creating the ground rules, they are much more likely to stick to them.

The act of setting ground rules gives participants a chance to think about the best way to behave in a workshop situation. Ground rules also serve as a legitimate basis for participants to reprimand each other later on for inappropriate behaviour. This is particularly helpful for you, the facilitator, as it means you don't need to do it yourself. However, participants who step out of line do need to be spoken to, and it may eventually fall to the facilitator to do this even if you have set very clear ground rules. It may be that no one else is brave enough to address the problem.

Running open forum discussions

Open forum discussions have to be carefully managed to ensure that everyone contributes, and that the discussion is focused. Record comments on a flipchart or whiteboard as you go along. This is a good way to keep the discussion focused, and to maintain a clear record of what is being said. This can be done either by using a structured discussion tool, or by simply posing a good open question and recording ideas in list form or spider form (see Chapter 3 for examples of the use of tools and diagrams). Use the flipchart or whiteboard as a living representation of the discussion. Symbols or colours can be added to lists or diagrams to record the views of the participants. See Figure 4.1 for an example of a brainstorm that has been used as the basis for further discussion.

It is vital to involve all participants in an open forum discussion. This can be done by moving around the group in sequence and asking for comments. The workshop can get rather stilted and predictable if you use this method all the time. Alternate it with free-for-all discussions, remembering that if you run a free-for-all discussion you need to keep a mental note of who has not yet spoken and invite them to contribute. A gentle invitation could be 'Is anyone else still waiting to add to the list?' or more pointedly 'Paul, it would be good to get your views on this one.'

Listening and questioning skills are very important in open forum discussions. The facilitator has to listen to each contribution, clarify it, challenge it if necessary, and open the issue up for further discussion. If

How to make our service better

Cheaper   ☺
~~Smile more~~
Get there quicker
Offer extras
Carry more spares
More flexible with times   ☺
Mobile phones   ☺
Look professional
Ask them what they want   ☺
Feedback forms   ●   – people hate them
Clear up   – do this already
~~Air freshener~~
~~Bring a bunch of flowers~~
Give a free electrical survey   ☺
Offer to look at other things
Trade-in service for duff equipment   ●   – no storage area
Price catalogues
Pay by credit card   ☺
Fridge overhauls   ●   – no skills

☺   Most popular ideas
●   Least popular ideas
~~Idea~~   Rejected ideas

Figure 4.1   *Annotated brainstorm*

you are a novice facilitator, a useful rule of thumb is to always ask one follow-up question per participant contribution. This forces you to listen to the contribution, and will help you to clarify what has been said. (Note that you should not question brainstorm contributions on the first pass. These must be written up without comment. See Chapter 3 for a full description of brainstorming.)

Managing individual tasks

When individuals are set tasks, each party must be completely clear about what is expected. It is too easy to waste time while 12 individuals sit silently for ten minutes, all doing the wrong thing.

61

Give participants a specific task, a set time in which to complete the task and a crisp description of what you want them to produce. For example 'Spend ten minutes on this exercise. Think about your experiences of using the current system. Write down five things which you like about the current system, and five things which you dislike about it.' Check understanding by asking 'Is everyone clear about what I'm asking you to do?' Don't worry if this seems patronizing. It is a useful question.

During the task, wander round the group and glance unobtrusively over people's shoulders. Make sure they are doing the right thing. Give the participants a warning around one minute before time is up.

When the time is up, get everyone's attention and explain how you will take their views in the open forum. Prepare the flipchart so that contributions can be recorded clearly. In the above case, a balance sheet can be used to record contributions (see Chapter 3 for a description of a balance sheet). Figure 4.2 shows the balance sheet resulting from the above individual task.

Each time a contribution is made, the facilitator should press for clarity, and confirm understanding by agreeing the wording for the flipchart entry. Do not simply write up comments that you do not understand. For example:

Participant: 'One bad thing about the system is that it is completely unfriendly.'
Facilitator: 'Unfriendly?'
Participant: 'Yes. When there is a problem, you get these strange error messages.'
Facilitator: 'Shall I write *strange error messages*?'
Participant: 'Yes. That's my point exactly.'

Likes	Dislikes

Easy to use
Don't need to read the
    manual
Fast
Nice graphics
	Strange error messages
	Doesn't produce reminder
	    letters
	Falls over quite a lot

Figure 4.2   *Example balance sheet for recording individual task results*

Managing small group tasks

Small group tasks must also be completely clear. Group tasks have a greater chance of going off the rails than individual tasks, as there is more potential for one confused person to persuade another confused person to do something completely different.

Ask the participants to write down the instructions as you talk the task through, or give them typed-up instructions. Make sure they know what they have to do, how long they should spend on the task and what you expect them to end up with.

Divide a large group into small groups of three or four. Don't get the participants to choose the groupings, this wastes time and has little benefit. It is best to send each small group to a different quiet corner, so that the groups do not disturb each other. Try to get the group members to sit in a circle, rather than in a straight line at a table. People communicate more effectively with each other when they can see each other's eyes. The following serves as a sample set of instructions.

In your group of 4, please spend 30 minutes answering the following questions. Focus specifically on the man-machine interface facilities. Elect someone to write down your answers, and present them back to the group in summary form.

- *What new features would you like to see in the system?*
- *Which features of the old system would you like to keep?*
- *Which features of the old system would you like to say goodbye to?*

During the task, you should move between the groups, and sit in on their discussions. Only add your own comments if you think the group is going off track, or if they need some extra information to avoid getting stuck. Give them a warning a few minutes before time is up. When that time arrives, call the groups back to the plenary group and ask them to sit together in the groups. Explain how you will take their views in the open forum. Prepare the flipchart so that contributions can be recorded clearly.

In the above case, you could use three separate flipchart sheets. These should all be visible at once, so stick two to the walls (get some special tape for doing this), and leave the third on the flipchart stand.

Record the contributions as you go along. Don't let one group speak for too long – the others will get bored. Make sure all the groups contribute. In the above case you could ask each group representative to give you one contribution for each category, then move round each group, collecting items until you run out of contributions. Each time a contribution is made, the facilitator should press for clarity, and should confirm understanding by agreeing the wording for the flipchart entry. See the example given in the previous section.

Employing discussion tools

Structured discussion tools are discussed in full in Chapter 3. If you decide to make use of these tools, explain them first to the participants who may not be familiar with them. Don't use technical terms for the tools used; just introduce the concept, and explain what you want the participants to do. People sometimes react against gimmicky techniques. If tools are used with confidence, and in the correct situation, the discussion will be focused and constructive.

When you are learning, do not attempt to use too many unfamiliar tools at once. Break yourself in gently by practising one at a time. The workshop situation is a busy one; you have to listen, question, monitor contributions, keep to the topic, manage time and write things up on the flipchart. There is no extra time available for worrying about how a certain tool is really supposed to work!

Managing time

Manage the agenda in half-hour blocks with each block covering a specific area. Remember that if you overrun in one section, you will have to curtail another section. Keep an eye on the clock, and if it looks as if you will overrun by more than ten minutes on one section, tell the participants. They may then choose either to curtail the current discussion, or to carry on anyway, at the expense of another area. It is not a good idea to change the programme without telling the participants; they will find this disconcerting and may very well react negatively, even if the change is brilliantly conceived.

Interesting discussions should not be cut short for the sake of rigidly sticking to your pre-set agenda. However, you should try to keep to the basic structure of your plan, and may sometimes need to be firm about which parts of the agenda are negotiable and which are not.

STOP AND THINK!

Question 5

What do you do if three out of the ten workshop participants say they have to leave one hour earlier than planned?

Question 6

In a workshop on company vision for Bilvo Plc, you set a small group exercise that involves the group spending 15 minutes coming up with a list of unique Bilvo Plc company characteristics. As you wander around the groups after five minutes, you find that three groups are doing as you asked, while the fourth group is creating a list of all comparable companies and for each company they are identifying a unique selling point. What do you do?

Question 7

You set a ten-minute individual exercise, and realize that after five minutes that one participant is still sitting with a blank piece of paper, staring into space. She has not even picked up her pencil. What do you do?

Capturing and using workshop data

Workshop data must be captured for two key reasons. These are:

- to act as a highly visible record of the workshop discussion as the workshop progresses;
- to provide a post-workshop report for the participants, the sponsor and any other stakeholders.

Workshop data are normally captured in two main ways. The first way is to write up comments, votes and contributions as you go along on a flipchart or a whiteboard. The second way is to ask a scribe to take minutes. The first method is an essential part of running a facilitated workshop, and the second way is an optional extra, depending on the complexity of the workshop.

Video and tape recordings can also be used to capture workshop data. These methods seem attractive, but trawling through video or tape recordings, picking out the salient comments is a lengthy and difficult process. The sound quality is often poor and participant contributions can easily be drowned out by coughing or chair squeaking.

Before the start of the workshop, the facilitator must decide who should record what information. Usually the flipcharts created during the workshop provide a sound basis for a workshop report. Some facilitators allocate a workshop scribe either as a backup, or to record any detailed, complex comments or decisions.

There are a number of arguments against having a workshop scribe.

- The scribe cannot take part in the workshop, as he or she will be too busy writing, which may be a loss.
- Being a scribe is quite a dull job and is difficult to do well. Scribes have been known to fall asleep!
- Much workshop discussion comprises people thinking out loud, playing devil's advocate or simply posturing. Although this is all useful stuff in the cut and thrust of the discussion, it is a waste of energy to record it all.
- Skilful use of structured workshop tools will enable the facilitator to record contributions and weight of feeling as the workshop progresses, so there should be no need for a scribe.

However, scribes are useful when:

- There is a lot of complex data to record, so having a scribe saves time.
- Important decisions are being made, and the scribe provides a backup record that acts as a fail-safe mechanism.

Handling difficult situations and difficult people

Running over time

If it looks as if the group discussion will overrun on a particular topic and the discussion is relevant and useful, you can either:

- stop the group and promise to return to the issue later if there is time, or
- explain that another section will be curtailed and negotiate a small overrun (eg 5–15 minutes).

However, if the discussion is drifting into personal bugbears or right off the subject of the workshop, the facilitator should bring participants back on track without destroying the relaxed atmosphere. The following should be tried:

I am concerned that time is short today, and as this topic is not strictly on the agenda I'll have to ask you to continue that conversation outside the workshop. Let's now continue with…

Another problem that consumes a lot of time in workshops is discussion that goes around in circles. This often happens when there are two polarized views of a situation, and each party tries to persuade the other party of the veracity of his or her view. If this continues beyond the point where useful progress is being made, the facilitator should move the group on to the next part of the agenda, while assuring participants that their views have been heard. The facilitator could try the following:

I think we have discussed this issue thoroughly, and are well aware of each other's views. When we allocate scores to these topics, you will get a chance to express your strength of feeling. Let's move on now to…

Hijack!

Sometimes a workshop participant will attempt to hijack your workshop and take control by changing the agenda, or by insisting that topics are covered in a different way. This normally happens near the start of a workshop, if it happens at all, and could be caused by any one of the following scenarios.

- The participant is used to taking control of a group, and is not good at sitting back.
- The participant has valid, important topics to place on the agenda, which you were unaware of.
- The participant wants to dominate the group to create an impression.
- The participant is expert in workshop facilitation and actually has a better idea.

My advice is to stick to your planned structure by using gentle persuasion, and to reassure people that they will get their say. Even if the participant is an expert facilitator, remember that you have been thinking about this workshop for weeks, while this person is coming on cold. It is very unlikely that the participant's approach will be markedly better than your approach, and it sets a bad precedent to completely alter your structure at the start of the workshop. It may open the flood-gates!

If there really are some totally new topics to be added to the agenda, then write them up, discuss them briefly, and take a straw poll on the most important issues of the day. If there is a very dominant member in the group, it might be advisable to allow people to vote in secret.

Blameless groups

When you are running a workshop which involves getting a work group to analyse, discuss and solve a problem, the group may have a tendency to blame outsiders for all their problems, and wish to avoid being self-critical.

This can be very frustrating, especially if part of your brief as facilitator is to get the group to focus on improving their internal processes. A good technique for overcoming this problem is to physically separate internal problems from external problems. This can be done by using two separate flipchart sheets to gather the two sets of problems. This technique gives participants a chance to air their grievances about outsiders, while encouraging them to focus on their own problems.

It is also important for individuals in blameless groups to be able to give their views about internal problems privately. This is because the group culture may be such that it is not acceptable to be self-critical. Private suggestions can be given on sheets of paper or on yellow stickers completed by each individual and stuck on the large flipchart sheet headed 'Internal problems'.

Energy too low

When the workshop energy is too low, participants seem unwilling to contribute, and enthusiasm fades. Low energy in a workshop can be caused by:

- lack of variation in activity;
- lack of involvement;
- lack of clarity about the topic in question;
- lack of belief that this workshop will make a difference;

- low-energy facilitator;
- aimless discussion;
- participants in need of drink, food or comfort break;
- room too hot;
- room too cold.

Low energy almost always occurs during the 'graveyard' shift, as it is widely known. The graveyard shift is the one-hour period after lunch during which participants may become sluggish and sleepy due to blood-sugar levels. This effect becomes even more obvious after a heavy lunch or consumption of alcohol, so try to ensure that participants avoid wine, beer or bread and butter pudding!

Low energy can usually be counteracted by either changing the activity to something more specific and involving, or by taking a break. On the activity side, prescriptive small group work with a clear outcome works well after lunch. However, if participants have physical needs that are concerning them, have a ten-minute break to allow people to walk around, and see to their own particular needs. I have heard of workshops that go on for four hours without any breaks, change of activity, or any sign of lunch at the usual hour. This is daft macho nonsense. It is impossible for human beings to operate at maximum capacity for that length of time.

If your subject matter is dull, then pep it up with a variety of interesting exercises. Never use the subject matter as an excuse for low energy. A creative facilitator can make even the dullest topics stimulating and involving. Read the section below on Body language to find out how you can spot low energy in its early stages.

Energy too high

High-energy workshops can be great fun, but have to be carefully directed. A high-energy workshop in which participants are focused and involved is not a problem, whereas a high-energy workshop in which participants are becoming unruly is definitely a problem.

Although high-energy workshops rarely get out of hand, the signs that things have gone far enough are:

- people chatting loudly about an unconnected topic;
- participants sharing obscure jokes;
- participants making fun of each other;
- participants making fun of the facilitator (to be avoided!).

69

You know that the energy is flowing in the right direction when participants become involved in animated discussions about the topic in question during the coffee breaks. The energy is flowing in the wrong direction when participants don't seem to be concentrating on the task in hand, but are none the less quite vocal.

Misdirected high energy may result from one of the following problems:

● boredom;
● lack of involvement;
● lack of clarity about the topic in question;
● lack of belief that this workshop will make a difference;
● high-energy facilitator who lacks focus;
● high-energy facilitator who allows the group too much control.

Unruly workshops can be brought under control by giving participants a highly active task to complete, which has a clear focus. Ringleaders should be split up into separate groups. Mini-presentations are especially useful, as they demand a high level of participation, and force participants to structure and vocalize their views. See Chapter 3 for a full description of this technique.

Poor brief

In the case where you have been asked to facilitate a workshop for a particular manager, you may find yourself facing a workshop situation that is quite different from the one you expected. There are a number of problems which could confront you:

● Participants have not had access to important information, which you were told they had seen.
● Participants have not completed pre-workshop tasks.
● Participants do not have the background, job role or experience that you expected.
● Participants are expecting a different workshop altogether.
● Participants have been told an incorrect finishing time.
● Participants say they have already covered this topic in a previous workshop.

It is wise to ask as many questions as you can about the participants and the topic beforehand. However, there are some items in the list above that are unavoidable, and must be handled as they arise. Each item is addressed below.

Pre-workshop information

Bring as much information with you as possible, and check at the start of the workshop whether the participants have seen the documents you're expecting them to have seen. If anyone has missed out, you can fill the gaps.

Pre-workshop preparation

You should only expect 50 per cent of your participants to complete any pre-workshop task. Some participants will arrive early and try to complete the task in the ten minutes before the workshop begins. This is unsatisfactory, but better than nothing. Short of threats and other such skulduggery, there is no known way to make participants do the preparation required. It is worth asking for preparation to be done none the less, as it will save time during the workshop when those who have prepared help and inform those who have not.

Unexpected participants

If a participant arrives unexpectedly, make him or her feel welcome. Be flexible. Just because they are unexpected, it does not mean that they are useless!

Find out who this person is and what he or she knows. Explain the workshop aims and structure, and try to help the person to identify whether he or she has a valid contribution to make. If the person does have a valid contribution to make then there is no problem. If not, it is best if the person leaves.

Participants expecting something different

If all participants have a very different expectation of the workshop content, possibly due to a misleading memo they were sent beforehand, you can do one of two things.

- Explain what you have planned, and why it was thought to be useful in the hope of persuading participants to stick to the plan.
- Open the workshop plan up for negotiation, taking votes on topics to be addressed (for the more experienced facilitator only!).

Incorrect timings given to participants

If incorrect timings have been given to all participants, you may have to adjust your structure. If participants are expecting a longer workshop, this is relatively easy to deal with. You can allow the group to select specific topics for further in-depth discussion. If the participants are expecting a shorter workshop, you will have to negotiate with the group on which of your planned topics to leave in and which to exclude.

Repeat workshop

If participants have addressed the issue in question already in a different forum, then you need to find out exactly what was done before. This can be done by getting the group to split into twos and asking them to list what was covered in the previous workshop, and what is still to be discussed. If there are enough significant areas left to cover, you need to quickly map out a structure for the workshop. However, if there are no significant areas left to address, you should record the information generated by the participants and cancel the workshop.

Difficult individuals

Most participants are a delight to work with. However, sometimes one or two participants can cause problems in a workshop, and although this is the exception rather than the rule, it is best to be prepared. Typical difficult types of participants are listed below, together with some advice on how to deal with these people.

The manipulative workshop owner

Occasionally a manager will ask a facilitator to run a workshop with a pre-determined outcome or a hidden agenda. Pre-determined outcomes require manipulation of the participants, unless by luck they all agree with the set outcome. This can cause anger and frustration, when the participants realize the workshop is a sham. Groups usually spot hidden agendas, and this strategy may cause the participants to react negatively, especially on sensitive issues. Avoid these two situations by persuading the commissioning manager to tackle pre-determined outcomes or hidden agendas in a more open, honest way.

The overpowering workshop owner

If the workshop owner insists on attending the workshop, he or she may end up dominating the session (possibly inadvertently). The workshop owner, who tends to be a senior member of staff, will often express strong opinions about the topic in question. This has the effect of gagging the participants, which in turn has the effect of making the owner feel he or she has to say even more. It becomes a vicious circle. Therefore it is best to restrict the workshop owner's input either to the introductory section, or to wrap-up. If the owner insists on attending the workshop, brief him or her carefully beforehand, by explaining how much input is required.

The know-all

The presence of a real expert may have an inhibiting effect on the group. The facilitator should control this effect by asking the expert to keep quiet for a while, but specifically asking him or her at particular points in the discussion to evaluate what has been said so far.

A participant who dominates the session by assuming the expert role without foundation should be told that the views of everyone are sought. If this does not work, the person should be curtailed in mid-sentence if he/she goes on too long.

Persistent splinter groups

If participants chat in small splinter groups during large group discussions, you must let them know immediately that this is not acceptable. It is irritating and insulting to others. Explain that it is necessary to give everyone airtime, and to respect the opinions of others by listening to them. If the chatting continues, you can either become more blunt, or split the large group up for a small group task in such a way that the splinter group is broken up.

Shy individuals

Usually one or two workshop participants do not contribute at all in a big group discussion. These people will contribute more easily in small groups, where airtime is easier to come by. Do not bring shy people in with a brutal 'You're quiet over there!' This will make things worse by making the person feel humiliated as well as shy. However, round-robin discussion tools, which involve moving one at a time around the group, will ensure that the more reserved members are included in the discussion without being forced to fight for a moment to speak.

Antagonistic individuals

Antagonistic individuals pop up in workshops from time to time. They argue with all the points raised, express negative views and indicate that the whole exercise is a waste of time. The antagonistic participant should be addressed patiently to begin with, but if he or she is starting to consume more than his or her fair share of airtime, you will have to be explicit about this. If the behaviour continues, you should talk to the person in private and ask him or her either to be more constructive or to leave the workshop. On no account should you allow disruptive behaviour to continue.

Body language

Noticing workshop body language is vital to the success of the workshop. Participants do not always say whether they are happy or unhappy, clear or unsure, interested or bored, calm or frustrated. Therefore any additional information about the state of mind of participants gleaned through body language is extremely useful for giving the facilitator pointers about which questions to ask, which areas to clarify or when to change activity.

The examples given below should not be taken as hard and fast rules, but should be used in context with what is being said by participants, to access a situation.

Hand and arm gestures

Hand gestures can give clear pointers to the way a person is feeling, but because several gestures are quite similar, these need to be carefully noted. A few common ones appear below.

- *Nose rubbing, eye rubbing or hand over the mouth* – this indicates that the person is uncertain about what is being said, or is uncertain about what someone else is saying. If several participants are doing this while you speak, you need to clarify what you are saying and support your case with facts. If the hand to face gestures continue, you need to ask the participants what their concerns are.
- *Ear rubbing* – this indicates that the person has heard enough. If a number of participants are doing this, you know that a particular speaker has gone on too long, and should be curtailed. Pulling the ear forward indicates a desire to speak. This is a good way of knowing when a participant wants to make a contribution, even though he or

she might be having trouble finding a moment to speak. As facilitator, you can step in and gently invite the person to contribute by saying, for instance, 'You look as if you have something to add here, Simon'.

- *Neck scratch with index finger* – this indicates doubt or uncertainty. If you are trying to get a decision and one or two participants are doing this you might choose to air their concerns.
- *Neck rub* – this indicates discomfort with what is being said. When preceded by a slap, this indicates frustration or anger. When the latter sequence occurs, the facilitator needs to take action to ensure that any difficulties are aired.
- *Head resting fully on hand* – this indicates boredom. Change the activity or make the current activity more stimulating and involving.
- *Hand on chin, with index finger pointed upwards along the cheek* – this indicates that the person is listening, and considering the pros and cons of what is being said. This is a perfectly good state of mind for workshop participants to be in. It is a good sign.
- *Chin touching* – this indicates that the person is making a decision about what is being said. This is a good sign because it shows that the participant is paying attention, and taking what is being said seriously.
- *Hands clenched on the table, or raised up with elbows on the table* – this indicates that the person is feeling frustrated or hostile. The higher the clenched hands, the worse the frustration or hostility. Get the person to speak to air their views.
- *Arms folded* – this indicates that the person wishes to cut himself or herself off from the situation. It is a defensive or negative posture. Try to involve the person in constructive activity or discussion.
- *Hands behind head, arms above shoulders and elbows pointed out* – this indicates that the person is feeling very comfortable on this subject area. It may also indicate arrogance.

If a participant is making this last gesture it usually indicates that he or she wishes to have his or her experience in this area recognized. You can do this by saying for instance 'You have a lot of experience in this area, don't you Sheila? What are your views on this topic?' Usually at this point, the participant's arms will come down, and he or she will once again become part of the group. If the gesture continues, it will separate that individual from the group psychologically, and you will lose that person's contribution.

If the whole group is exhibiting the last gesture (and this often happens) then you know that the discussion has now become rather self-congratulatory, and thus not very constructive. This is a good time to change the activity and move on.

Leg positions

- *Legs crossed with feet down* – this is fairly normal position, and should not be taken to mean anything on its own. The direction of leg cross can however be significant. If legs are crossed towards someone, this indicates good rapport. Legs crossed away indicates the opposite. This is useful when monitoring small group activity, and will tell you how well the individuals are relating to each other.
- *Legs crossed, with one ankle resting on one knee* – this indicates an argumentative frame of mind. If a participant is sitting in this position, he or she is mentally debating what is being said. There is no problem with this, unless he or she appears to be disagreeing with everything that is said as a matter of course. If a participant is becoming over argumentative, he or she may have to be spoken to quietly during the break. The other possibility is to involve the participant in some responsible activity, such as giving a mini-presentation. This will provide an opportunity for him or her to be more constructive.
- *Feet crossed, ankles together* – this gesture indicates that the person is feeling defensive or is holding back a negative feeling such as anger, or frustration, or fear. When bosses and subordinates are mixed together in a workshop, you may notice the subordinates crossing their feet. This indicates that they are holding back, or are feeling defensive. This tells you that the discussion is not open and honest, and that secret voting may be necessary to gather views.

Extracting workshop actions

During the workshop it may be necessary to action individuals either to address an important issue or to do a specific task. Actions are best handled by sticking a large sheet of paper up on the wall, and writing the actions down in bold letters as you go along. Actions should only be given to those present at the workshop. If an issue needs to be addressed by someone outside the workshop, get a workshop participant to commit to doing something specific about it, for example writing a memo, or talking to an individual.

Important issues arising

Issues sometimes arise in a workshop which are important but cannot be dealt with by the workshop group because of lack of time, because the right people are not present or because the issue does not lie strictly within the workshop remit. The facilitator should note the issue on a sheet of flipchart paper or a whiteboard clearly marked 'Issues'. This enables participants to raise issues, but ensures that the workshop does not get sidetracked unnecessarily.

The issue list should be revisited at the end of the workshop to ensure that the right people get to know about the issues of concern, either via the post-workshop report or by giving actions to specific participants to follow issues up with people outside the workshop.

Making decisions

If the workshop purpose is to make important decisions then this should be done carefully. The rules for decision making should be crystal clear, so that no arguments arise afterwards. Examples of typical workshop decision making rules appear below.

If participants must select from a number of choices:

- the option with the highest number of votes wins, whatever the proportion of votes;
- the option with the highest number of votes wins only if more than 50 per cent of the participants vote for that option;
- the option with the highest number of votes wins only if more than 80 per cent of the participants vote for that option.

If the decision involves a straightforward 'yes' or 'no' to a particular proposal:

- the proposal is ratified if over 50 per cent of the participants say 'yes';
- the proposal is ratified if over 80 per cent of the participants say 'yes';
- the proposal is ratified if no one says 'no' (silence if compliance).

If the workshop atmosphere is open and honest, then open voting is fine. Otherwise secret voting is essential (see Chapter 3). When you are using open voting, be especially aware of the 'silence is compliance' rule, often used in decision making workshops. This can be counter-productive if dominant managers are present. Some participants may feel intimidated into remaining silent, when they might have quite strong (and well-informed) views. It may also fail to catch the views of the more reflective participants who may simply need more time to consider the options.

Closing the workshop

The facilitator closes the workshop formally by gathering the whole group together and running through what was covered and what was said. Particular care should be taken at this point to summarize all views given, rather than to concentrate only on the views of the majority or those of the most vocal participants.

Clarity about what happens next is important. If actions have been set, then the facilitator should arrange for an action list to be typed up and circulated. Notes that summarize what was said are normally typed up and circulated too – otherwise this information is lost. Clear concise notes help participants, and those not present at the workshop, to reflect on and analyse the information gathered. A follow-up meeting should also be arranged if appropriate.

STOP AND THINK!

Question 8

You are running a workshop that aims to get a group of six users to evaluate a prototype computer system. You begin to demonstrate the system, but as you look around at the group, one member who is a key user is sitting looking out of the window with his head resting firmly on his hand. What do you do?

Question 9

You are facilitating a workshop that is intended to gather the views of ten project managers on how the Project Management procedures in the company could be improved. Your first activity is to work as a large group, getting the group to list all the good and bad points of the current procedure. As you are asking for contributions, you notice that two of the project managers have a list of their own which they are filling in together. They are ignoring the rest of the group activity. What do you do?

Question 10

You have just come to the end of a very constructive and stimulating one-day workshop that has resulted in some key decisions being made about how to run the customer services. However, two of the Business Managers present, who are both vital to the successful implementation of the proposed changes, are sitting with their arms folded. What do you do?

—————— CHAPTER 5 ——————

The workshop environment

To have his path made clear for him is the aspiration of every human being in our beclouded and tempestuous existence.
Joseph Conrad

You may think that a facilitator's job is confined to the intellectual side of the process, such as researching the content and planning the workshop. However, the physical workshop environment is also very important. The facilitator can make a huge difference to the smooth running of the workshop by making the environment agreeable and conducive to constructive discussion.

If you are used to running events with groups of people, then much of this section will be familiar ground for you. If not, then read on, and make a mental checklist of all the relevant things you need to remember to address.

The workshop environment needs to be right to enable the workshop to run with maximum effectiveness. All the environmental factors listed below should be thought through and planned out in advance. You are very much on show when you are facilitating a workshop, and it pays to get things right.

Location

Many organizations have their own conference rooms. If you hold a workshop on-site you run the risk of multiple interruptions from desperate (or lazy) colleagues who would probably manage perfectly well if the participants were inaccessible. You also run the risk of participants returning to their desks in the breaks and getting sucked back into work issues. Try to run the workshop off-site, or be very strict about interruptions and return times (see pages 84 and 85).

Use an airy, light room with plenty of fresh air and a good ambient temperature. Distant views from the workshop window are especially conducive to creative, long-term thinking. However, if you have no choice and find yourself stuck in a hot, dingy, windowless room, beware; you will have to make the workshop extra stimulating to get the best out of the participants.

Equipment

Simple equipment is all that is usually necessary for a workshop. This means:

- flipchart with paper, pens and special tape, or
- overhead projector and pens, or
- whiteboard with pens and board cleaner.

The easiest, most flexible piece of equipment is the flipchart. It is perfect for a workshop of up to around 12 people as everyone can see what is being written, and the paper can be ripped off, stuck on the walls with special tape, and kept as a record of the workshop. The only problem with flipcharts is that you have to:

write larger than normal!

Test out your writing before the workshop begins by writing something up and walking around the workshop area to make sure that your writing is legible from a distance.

An overhead projector is good for presenting material, but is not so good for recording what is said. If your hands shake for whatever reason while you are writing they will be on view in magnified form to all present. Additionally, if the overhead projector is a standard machine, you will find yourself staring at a transparency with a bright light beneath. This is likely to give you a bad headache. Writing onto over-head transparencies is also prone to error as you can't lean on the projector, and the material is too smooth and slippery. If you do have to write on an overhead projector, check that your writing is large enough and legible enough for participants to read. Do this before the workshop begins. You also need to check the overhead projector focus before you start, rather than waste time fiddling about while people are waiting.

Whiteboards are good for recording limited amounts of information. They are especially good for spider diagrams (see Chapter 3 for a description of a spider brainstorm) because parts of the diagram can be erased and redrawn any number of times. If you are lucky enough to have access to the expensive type of whiteboard that can make copies of itself, you can copy whiteboard information on to paper, erase it from the whiteboard and carry on.

There is one special word of warning when using whiteboards; check the pen first! It is very easy to mix flipchart pens up with whiteboard pens, and find yourself with permanent writing on the whiteboard (special cleaning fluids do exist, but are rarely close at hand). This can be especially embarrassing when you are running a workshop that is dealing with confidential material. So test the pens out on a corner of the board to make sure that they can be erased.

Seating

Workshops are cosier and more intimate without a table because the table acts as a barrier between the participants. However, the table serves the practical purpose of providing something to lean on when writing, and with groups who are not familiar with each other it provides the necessary psychological protection.

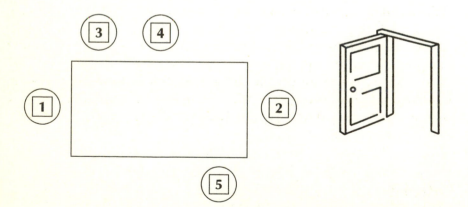

Figure 5.1 *Workshop seating arrangements*

Participants should all sit around one table, so that they can see each other's eyes. Do not allow any second or third rows to build up, as this will create an underclass in the workshop group. Clear eye contact is important for good group communication. A round table is best, but rather difficult to get hold of. Rectangular tables are fine, but seating positions then become more significant (see Figure 5.1).

The normal seating arrangements for a facilitated workshop is a rectangular table. You may have attended hundreds of workshops or meetings in the past, innocently believing that there is no significance to seating positions. However, you might be interested to know that the dynamics of a group can radically alter depending on who sits where.

Who normally sits at the head of the table facing the door at meetings in your organization? Is it the 'boss' or maybe someone who would like to be boss? Think back to your childhood days. Who sat at the top of the dinner table, facing the door? It was probably the head of the family. Without becoming too psychologically deep, the facilitator should maintain an awareness of, and possibly some influence over who sits where.

Study the seating position in Figure 5.1. They are numbered in order of associated power and influence:

1. The most influential position is at the end of the table, facing the door.
2. The second most influential position is at the opposite end of the table to number 1. Numbers 1 and 2 face each other directly, so may well find themselves in conflict.
3. The third most influential position is the nearest person to number 1.

If the facilitator has a difficult group to cope with, he or she should sit in position 1, facing the door, with an ally in position 2. If there is a known troublemaker in the group, that person should be encouraged to sit in any position except 1 or 2.

You can use name cards to encourage people to sit in prescribed seats, but this does set a rather over-structured tone for the workshop. People can always be moved around by setting small group tasks that involve new groupings.

Safety

Make sure that any equipment you use is safe. Common problems include tripping over overhead projector cables, being trapped by collapsing flipchart stands and falling prey to unstable overhead projectors. Overhead projector cables should be taped down with bright tape. Flipchart stands and overhead projector cables should be tested before the workshop for general stability.

It is a good idea (and it is usually the law) to ensure that the participants are aware of the fire exit route in the event of a fire. Find the relevant instructions, which are normally pinned to the door of the room and explain these to participants.

Food and drink

Food and drink should arrive on time, as promised, and should not be left to get cold or stew. A buffet meal is better than a sit down meal, as it helps the group to maintain its pace. Sit down meals can be quite slow and formal, especially in a hotel environment.

If you choose a buffet meal, that is fine, but do not expect people to contribute to the conversation while they are choosing or eating food. This is fundamental stuff! Take a break.

Heavy, stodgy food will slow people's thinking down. Lean food and plenty of fruit are more appropriate. Avoid alcohol as it makes people sleepy.

Breaks

Breaks should be taken when promised, so that people can do whatever they had planned in the break (for example make a quick call to the office). If a break is going to be late, the facilitator should tell the participants in advance so that they can make the necessary arrangements, such as visit the loo now! Late breaks are very irritating, especially for participants who have heavy schedules and many people who need to get in touch with them.

Group-work areas

If you choose to have some small group work in your programme, make sure that there is somewhere for the small groups to go. Simple small group activities can be done in the main meeting room, but longer, more involved tasks should be done with each group in a separate area. Groups get distracted if they can hear each other's discussions.

Most hotels or conference facilities have open areas where groups can sit to carry out any tasks allocated to them. However, be careful, also, of asking groups to discuss sensitive or complex issues in the public area of a hotel or conference facility. This will stifle openness and risk talking.

If you do not have the luxury of breakout rooms, which are obviously the ideal solution, make sure that each group has a flipchart with pens to work with.

Interruptions

Contain interruptions to the workshop session by installing a system to trap messages which you administer yourself. A simple one is to ask people outside the workshop to leave any messages in a large envelope attached to the workshop door. You gather the messages during the break and distribute them to participants. Check your system out with participants, and clear it with local administrative people.

Sometimes workshop participants assume that it is quite all right to drift in and out of the workshop as the mood takes them. This notion should be discouraged, preferably at the ground rule stage, as it is distracting for those who stay, causes time-wasting repetition and gives a disjointed feel to the workshop.

Mobile phones and pagers

Make clear at the start of the workshop that mobile phones and pagers should only be used during the breaks. Ask participants to switch their machinery off during the sessions, and explain that this makes the workshop more worthwhile for everyone.

Pens and paper

Most well-travelled workers will bring their own pen and paper to a workshop, but there are always a few who do not. You should ensure you provide enough pens for everyone and enough paper for any amount of scribbling.

Name cards or badges

If workshop participants are not familiar with each other, then it is a good idea to come up with some system that helps them to remember each other's names. This allows the workshop communication to flow better and the group to gel more quickly, which is especially important if the workshop is to run over several days. Badges are ideal, but name cards can work. The only problem with name cards in a workshop is that people move around so much that the desk-bound name card becomes ineffective.

STOP AND THINK!

Question 1

Your boss suggests that the workshop you are running for senior management should be held in the in-house conference room, so that people can be pulled out easily to attend to any urgent problems. What do you say?

Question 2

You arrive at a workshop and the seating is in café style. This means that there are five small circular tables, each one with four chairs around it. You have 16 participants and there is no extra furniture. What do you do and why?

Question 3

You are running a workshop to generate ideas for a new product. You have been warned about one participant in particular who has been working on the existing product for 25 years, and can see nothing wrong with it. He is very antagonistic to this new development. He sits down at the opposite end of the table from you, with his back to the door (the equivalent of position 2 in Figure 5.1). Do you move him? If so, why and how? If not, why not?

CHAPTER 6

What to do afterwards

Light tomorrow with today!
Elizabeth Barrett Browning

A facilitated workshop should make a difference! Effective workshops are part of a larger process, so after the workshop is finished the workshop results should be quickly and clearly communicated to everyone who needs to know. The best way of doing this is to produce a concise, accurate written report.

It is important to avoid the scenario in which a group of participants attends an interesting workshop, contributes enthusiastically, and then nothing appears to happen. If no report appears, participants will assume that their efforts were in vain and that it was all a waste of time. Management will assume that it was just another talking shop, and other employees not involved in the workshop will either assume that these workshops lead to nothing or that some Machiavellian plot is being hatched. This will not do future workshops any good at all.

The contents of the post-workshop report should be clearly thought out before the workshop begins. Will you record everything that is said? Will you identify who voted which way in the report? Are you looking to capture any specific data (quantitative or qualitative)?

The nature of the information required from the workshop will affect the workshop organization and atmosphere. If the plan is to record and circulate a verbatim record of who said what, then the workshop will require a scribe and people will be fairly careful about what they say. However, if the plan is to record lists of ideas and voting proportions without names attached, then a scribe will not be needed and the discussion will probably be more fluid and open. In the latter case, discussion tools should be used to organize the discussion and record views (see Chapter 3 for a description of a range of discussion tools).

Informing participants

Participants should get a copy of the workshop report. This is often forgotten, as facilitators and sponsors assume that because the participants were there, they have no need to see the report. However, participants will want to know how the workshop output has been represented to other parties, and what is going to change as a result of the workshop. If the workshop is part of a series, participants will also want to know what is happening at the other workshops, and how the views of others compare with their own views. This will help participants to understand the wider picture, and therefore to accept any resulting decisions that are made that are different from ones they recommended.

Informing the workshop sponsor

The workshop sponsor will want to know what was discussed, what was decided, what ideas were generated and what concerns were aired. The facilitator should take care to preserve any confidentiality agreements with participants, especially if secret voting techniques were used. It is often more useful to report the views of the workshop as a whole rather than the particular opinions of individuals, which the sponsor could glean by one-to-one conversations if he or she wanted to.

Informing other parties

Other parties may also be interested in the output of a workshop. Think carefully about what information might be useful to whom. Sensitive information needs to be carefully packaged to avoid misinterpretation or imaginative speculation.

Reporting back

The facilitator should produce a clear report after the workshop that encapsulates:

● what was covered in the workshop;

- the structure of the discussion;
- how the discussion went;
- the broad timing of the session;
- ideas generated;
- evaluations generated;
- diagrams created;
- voting results;
- decisions made;
- actions arising;
- issues arising.

The report should be clear and concise, rather than a turgid mass of dense impenetrable prose. The facilitator's opinions should not be part of the report, and the contents of the report should be restricted to facts rather than conjecture (as much as is humanly possible). A covering note should be attached, tailored to the relevant recipient (participant, sponsor, etc), which explains what has happened so far and what the next steps are.

Quantitative workshop data are easier to report than qualitative workshop data, being easy to capture and easy to represent. Give a clear context for all quantitative data presented, and explain any terms or codes used. Your original flipchart notes may have to be expanded to make the report clear for those who were not present at the workshop.

An extract from a workshop report appears below in Extract A which illustrates how quantitative data can be reported. This report resulted from a workshop that aimed to find out what participants thought of the company appraisal system.

Extract A

The workshop comprised nine participants. After much discussion, the group settled on a list of eight improvement characteristics of an effective company appraisal system.

The participants then considered the current appraisal system and decided individually which of these characteristics were present, and which were not. They were given the option of Yes, No or ? (don't know) in an open voting session.

Ratings for current appraisal system

Characteristic	Yes	No	?
Enhances communication between manager and individual	9	0	0
Enabled good quality feedback on performance	7	2	0
Clarifies work objectives	3	6	0
Enables career planning	3	5	1
Clarifies learning objectives	5	4	0
Contributes to training plan	2	5	2
Influences staff member's next project	1	8	0
A chance to air gripes and be listened to	6	3	0

Qualitative data are harder to report, as they may consist of issues raised, level of concern expressed or duration and emphasis of discussion. Quantitative measures can be used to give substance to qualitative data. For instance, the appraisal workshop report referred to above also contained the extract shown below in Extract B. This extract seeks to express qualitative data, using numbers to add clarity.

Extract B

The discussion on career planning was the most heated and extended. While other items on the list took ten minutes to cover, the career planning part took 30 minutes. Six out of the nine participants took part energetically in this discussion. Two participants in particular felt very strongly that careers were not addressed in appraisals, and could cite instances where their own requests for particular career-enhancing job moves had not been acted upon. Two participants felt that the system had enhanced their careers by providing good opportunities at the right time.

Dealing with workshop actions

Actions arising from the workshop should be listed clearly in the workshop report. Express each action in an unambiguous way, with a note of who is responsible for carrying the action out, and by when. As with any meeting, it is not a good idea to record an action against anyone who was not present because you have not got his or her consent. However, you can action someone who was at the workshop to talk to the person in question.

Take care to ensure that actions are recorded, allocated and distributed, but you do not necessarily have to take responsibility for checking up on everyone, unless you are their manager, of course. If not, do not be tempted to become the group's nanny! Ensure that actions are followed up, preferably by the workshop sponsor.

Dealing with issues arising

Issues that arose in the workshop but could not be dealt with should be followed up with the workshop sponsor. In an ideal world, the sponsor's response to the issues would be included in the workshop report. However, this often causes delay in producing the report, which can slow down the wider process of dealing with particular problems, pursuing new ideas or making necessary improvements.

List the issues arising in the workshop report, together with any relevant information about who will follow the issue up or what the sponsor intends to do about the particular issue.

What next?

Participant: 'That was excellent. I think we really made progress. So what happens next?'

Facilitator: 'Yes, it went very well. My job now is to put all the recommendations together in a report by the end of this week. All the participants, the sponsor and the senior management team will have a copy of my report by Monday. The sponsor will be using this information together with the output from the other four workshops to make decisions about how to progress. She is meeting with the senior management team on Wednesday to specifically discuss the issue, and she has promised to send out an e-mail to all participants regarding the next steps on Thursday.'

Participants will be keen to know what happens next, especially if they have contributed enthusiastically during the workshop. If you can

91

give a detailed, direct response like the one above, that is ideal. Unfortunately, I have overheard some far less helpful replies such as 'I'm not sure, I'm just the facilitator' or 'It's over to the Senior Managers now. You'll just have to wait and see what happens.' Plan your response to this question as someone is bound to ask it, and give as much detail as possible.

Example reports

Two examples of workshop reports appear below. Example A shows how qualitative and quantitative data can be used together to create a good, concise record of the workshop. Example B illustrates how to confuse, irritate and misinform all at once! Too many data are presented in some parts, and not enough in others. The process is not clearly explained, and the report is then overlaid with opinions and conjecture.

Example A

To: All workshop participants
From: Diane Jones
Subject: Appraisal Scheme Workshop Report
Date: March 18

CC: Yvonne Stewart, Mike Thurston, Jane Sullivan

I enclose the workshop report as promised. This has been sent to Yvonne Stewart, Mike Thurston and Jane Sullivan, who will be deciding on what changes to make to the system by the end of April. You will receive an e-mail from Jane before then, explaining what they intend to do and why. If you have any queries about the contents of this report, please call me on extension 242 at the Hull office.

The Appraisal Scheme Workshop was held in the main Hull office on 16 March from 09.00 until 12.00. There were nine participants, selected by picking every tenth staff member from the alphabetical staff list. The participants formed a representative group of staff. See characteristics below:

Person 1	Hull office	Sales Manager	5 years' service
Person 2	Manchester office	Office Manager	2 years' service
Person 3	Hull office	Sales Representative	2 years' service
Person 4	Edinburgh office	Technical Grade 2	1 years' service
Person 5	Manchester office	Receptionist	8 years' service
Person 6	Hull office	Technical Grade 7	5 years' service
Person 7	Hull office	Technical Grade 5	3 years' service
Person 8	Manchester office	Technical Grade 5	2 years' service
Person 9	Edinburgh office	Sales Representative	4 years' service

The purpose of the workshop was to find out what the group thought about the effectiveness of the appraisal system, and what aspects of it they thought could be improved.

The first hour was spent discussing and deciding what the most important characteristics of an effective appraisal system were. The discussion became quite heated over the issue of career planning which over half the group thought was a problem within the organization. Six out of the nine people present could cite two or three different instances when staff had left the company because of a lack of response to requests for particular career opportunities. Other topics on the list (see below) were covered easily in ten minutes. The group were all very positive about the clarity of the feedback given via the appraisal system.

The group then agreed on the eight most important characteristics of an effective appraisal system. This list appears below together with the results of a secret vote, which asked each individual to allocate ten votes across all the listed characteristics according to how well the company system did on each characteristic.

Ratings for current appraisal system

Characteristics	Points
Enhances communication between manager and individual	30
Enables good quality feedback on performance	45
Clarifies work objectives	5
Enables career planning	5
Clarifies learning objectives	0
Contributes to training plan	0
Influences staff member's next project	0
A chance to air gripes and be listened to	5

- time to talk;
- manager;
- training;
- job;
- pause for thought;
- a chance to moan;
- development?;
- influence career;
- set objectives;
- find out what they think of you;
- give views;
- keep in touch;
- impress;
- depress!

After a process of discussion, with Tim and Hilary getting quite upset about the career issue (mostly because they feel their own careers are stagnating, which may or may not be the fault of the appraisal system), this list was whittled down to five. This was done by allocation of the following votes (each participant could allocate ten points amongst the list):

- time to talk JH(5) KJ(1);
- manager KJ(2);
- training JH(3) HT(4) JD(5) FG(7);
- job;
- pause for thought KJ(7) RW(2);
- a chance to moan RW(5);
- development?;
- influence career JH(2) HT(6) TB(6) RW(3) FG(3);
- set objectives;
- find out what they think of you LK(5) JD(3);
- give views LK(5) TB(4) JD(2);
- keep in touch;
- impress;
- depress! LP(10).

The five favoured issues were discussed, and the group came up with three key, workable recommendations. These are listed below, not in order of priority. I have excluded the less relevant suggestions about mentoring, staff councils and suggestion schemes.

- Sort out the career planning side, by implementing fixed career paths and assessment schemes.
- Training must improve. Have a yearly training plan, with a budget.
- Advertise what training is available, because staff do not know what can be done, and what cannot.

I think many participants were using this workshop as therapy. This is because some of these people are very rarely asked their opinion, so when they are asked they may overdo it! Thus some of the views should be taken with a pinch of salt.

STOP AND THINK!

Question 1

How should the facilitator report the results of a brainstorming session? Verbatim, paraphrased, summarized or not at all? Justify your answer.

Should the facilitator indicate in the report whether voting is open or secret, and if so why?

Should the facilitator put his or her personal views in the final workshop report? When might this be appropriate and when would it not be appropriate?

Question 2

List all the specific problems with the report in Example B above. How would you rectify these problems?

Question 3

A one-page workshop report arrives on your desk. It describes a workshop that you wanted to attend but could not because you were on holiday. This is an extract from the section that describes a discussion and decision making session regarding the visual end of a software system which you were involved in developing (often referred to as the Man-Machine Interface). Brian, Dave and Kate are all potential users of the system.

How would you react? How could things have been handled differently?

We ran a workshop last week for BLATT Plc, to discuss the Man-Machine Interface. Seven users were present. However, only Brian, Dave and Kate were really taking part in the discussion. This is how the discussion went:

Brian, the Business Accounts Manager, was very pleased with what we have done so far. Both he and Dave liked the colours and shapes, but Kate hated the yellow background! The icons were acceptable to everyone, although Sue thought they could be larger, and reckoned that the speed at which the menus popped up was too slow. Brian disagreed.

There was some discussion about the alarm sound that the computer makes if there is a problem in the control room. Kate thought it was a bit 'squeaky', whereas Brian thought it should be louder.

Dave thought that the look of the thing should be a bit more like the FFS system. Brian agreed.

All in all, no big problems.

CHAPTER 7

Other issues surrounding the use of workshops

This chapter comprises three sections. Each one addresses an issue that is peripheral to the practical business of running facilitated workshops, but is none the less extremely important in achieving long-term success.

The first section looks at how the workshop fits into the bigger organizational picture. This is of crucial importance to the effectiveness of the workshop in helping to achieve organizational goals. The second section addresses the thorny problems of who should facilitate a workshop. Should the facilitator be a familiar insider, or a fresh-faced outsider? The third and final section is about how to improve your facilitation skills. This section leads you through a proposed learning plan, and features a useful form for gleaning feedback from your colleagues.

Workshops as part of the organizational change process

Facilitated workshops can be used very effectively to catalyse and progress change within organizations. However, nasty surprises are in store for those who believe that an isolated series of workshops will achieve lasting change. The facilitated workshop serves to get people thinking, to gather ideas and to make decisions. Changes will only happen in reality when people start to do things differently, and this needs to be encouraged by supportive management action, procedural change, appropriate training, necessary resources, motivation rewards and the right organizational structure.

Organizational changes can be separated into two categories. Argyris (1992) called the first type 'single loop' change. This type of change involves a simple alteration to correct a problem, or makes an improvement to the way things are done. A good example of this type of change is an alteration to the company sales procedure which involves transferring from a paper based system to a new computerized system. This change would mean training the sales staff, and constructing a new procedure. There might be some resistance to the change, but with the right support and encouragement this type of change should not cause too many problems.

The second type is referred to by Argyris as 'double loop' change. Double loop change involves a deeper level of change, which necessitates not only changes in the working processes but also a fundamental change in attitudes. A good example of this is a change on a factory shop floor from working in supervised lines to working in autonomous teams. This change would involve changes in the physical environment to enable teams to work together and talk together, changes in management style, changes in supervisor attitudes, changes in team member skills and changes in the way work is done.

Single loop change can be achieved relatively easily in organizations where procedures are clear, and managers routinely involve staff in decision making activities. Simple single loop changes can be made difficult if the management style is to force changes through without consultation and fail to provide the necessary support. It is common knowledge now that those who have been involved early on in the process of change will always accept a change more willingly.

Workshops can provide a quick, effective tool to enable single loop change, by involving the right staff in deciding what will change, and giving staff an opportunity to work out how the changes can be assimilated and what support is needed. Using the above example of a change in the sales process, a workshop could be used to involve the sales people at one or all of the following stages in the change process:

- at the start – to evaluate and select from a range of possible computerized sales systems;
- when the system has been selected – to review the selected sales system and decide how it should be used and how to induct sales staff;
- when the draft procedure has been written – to review the new sales procedure and to recommend changes and decide what additional support is needed to make the new procedure work.

Double loop change is always harder to achieve because it involves making changes at the very heart of an organization, and organizations can be surprisingly resistant to fundamental changes.

For instance, attempts to introduce Total Quality Management principles into organizations in the 1980s failed in over 60 per cent of cases (Binney, 1992). One of the key reasons for this failure was the slavish reliance on facilitated workshops to solve company quality problems. These workshops were not well understood by management, and were therefore treated with, at best, a bemused tolerance or, at worst, suspicion and disdain. In many cases senior managers did not give the workshops the support they needed and eventually many of these initiatives simply fizzled out because those taking part in the workshops could see that their efforts were not making a difference. Therefore organizations using facilitated workshops as part of the double loop change must ensure that the workshops are supported by key managers to ensure success.

The ideal organizational structure is one in which change is normal, and facilitated workshops are used routinely to involve people in the various stages of changing and adapting the organization. Pedler, Burgoyne and Boydell (1996) established the idea of the Learning Company in their excellent book of the same name. The authors define a learning company as 'an organization that facilitates the learning of all its members and continuously transforms itself'. This ideal is well within the grasp of many small organizations, but quite a long way off for many large organizations. A good start on the road to developing a learning culture is to begin to use facilitated workshops as part of the decision making process. Staff will then begin to develop a culture of listening and learning from each other, and the whole organization will begin to communicate more freely.

Using external facilitators

When I run facilitation skills workshops for managers, consultants and internal facilitators, I am regularly asked my opinion on the use of external facilitators.

In an ideal world, companies would be able to do their own facilitation in all cases, because the organizational culture would be one of listening, learning and transforming. However, most normal organizations still have a long way to go to reach this ideal, and facilitation has to be done with care within the existing culture.

The use of external facilitators to run company workshops has some very clear advantages. The advantages of external facilitators are:

- they can challenge the status quo;
- they can bring in new information;
- they provide a fresh pair of eyes;
- they can help with benchmarking against other companies;
- they are less affected by the seniority of participants;
- they are seen as impartial.

However, the disadvantages of external facilitators are:

- they lack specific company knowledge;
- they may not get the respect of participants;
- they may be seen as not caring and not involved;
- they may misunderstand the company culture, and thus fail to enable changes to happen;
- they may be easily swayed by the paying client, who may have a hidden agenda.

External facilitators are therefore useful in facilitated workshops which:

- tackle difficult new territory;
- involve considering the external environment;
- do not demand in-depth company knowledge;
- involve conflict.

They are not so good for facilitated workshops which:

- focus on specific, detailed technical issues;
- involve unwilling participants;
- necessitate a highly detailed knowledge of existing company culture.

Internal facilitators have advantages and disadvantages too. In large organizations their distance from local issues and their ability to look afresh on a problem means that they can act in a very similar manner to an external facilitator. In small organizations, however, although they have good knowledge of the areas required, they can suffer from being too close to the problems and being seen as partisan.

Many managers choose to facilitate their own team workshops. This is of course the ideal and fits in very well with the learning company profile (see previous section in this chapter for an explanation). However, managers who facilitate their own team workshops need to ensure that their facilitation style is consistent with their management style. Staff will find it difficult to react to a manager who is dominant and controlling day in, day out, and who listens and consults only in the workshop environment.

Improving your facilitation skills

Once you have read through this book and completed the accompanying questions inserted in each section, you need to practise the skills in a real life situation. You cannot learn to juggle by reading a book alone. You need to start throwing some oranges around!

The learning process, first defined by Kolb (1984) and refined by many subsequent writers, shows the sequence of activities we go through in order to learn. The process is shown in Figure 7.1. It provides a useful illustration of how we learn from experience and reflection. If you start the learning process by reading a book such as this one, you have probably started to form some ideas about how you intend to approach facilitation. If you have already had some experience of running workshops, you have probably used the book to reflect on that experience and to form some new ideas. Whichever your starting point, your next step is to try out some of your new ideas.

Experience a real life event

**Test out new ideas
in new situations**

**Reflect on the experience
and make observations**

Form new ideas and theories

Figure 7.1 *The learning process*

I suggest that you follow the learning plan defined below over a period of about six months, setting aside time to write down your reflections, and planning your next step around concrete opportunities for practice.

If this is impractical because of time or work pressures, and you are being asked to run a full-blown workshop in a short time frame, then my advice is to start with something simple and work up to something more complex. Your first workshop should employ only a handful of discussion tools, and should specifically avoid splitting participants into groups as it increases the complexity. I do however recommend trying out the discussion tools on a tame audience before plunging in at the deep end with a real group of expectant participants. This will do wonders for your confidence, and your effectiveness. You should also take time after the event to reflect on how your workshops go, so that you are continually improving, rather than developing bad habits.

Learning plan

Learning step one: **Guide a standard meeting such as a progress meeting using a flipchart.**

- **What do I want to achieve?**
- **What did I achieve?**
- **What went well?**
- **What do I need to do differently next time?**

Learning step two: **Use a structured discussion tool to guide discussion at a meeting.**

- **What do I want to achieve?**
- **What did I achieve?**
- **What went well?**
- **What do I need to do differently next time?**

Learning step three: **Use a voting technique to make a decision at a meeting.**

- **What do I want to achieve?**
- **What did I achieve?**
- **What went well?**
- **What do I need to do differently next time?**

Learning step four: **Run one segment of a meeting as a mini-workshop, using two or three discussion tools to guide discussion and make a decision.**

- What do I want to achieve?
- What did I achieve?
- What went well?
- What do I need to do differently next time?

Learning step five: **Organize a half-day workshop to tackle an appropriate issue.**

- What do I want to achieve?
- What did I achieve?
- What went well?
- What do I need to do differently next time?

Learning step six: **Organize a half-day workshop, and begin to widen your variety of discussion tools, for instance using mini-presentations.**

- What do I want to achieve?
- What did I achieve?
- What went well?
- What do I need to do differently next time?

Once you begin to run full-blown facilitated workshops, you should encourage the participants to give you feedback on how you did. There is no such thing as a perfect workshop. You can always improve and hone your skills. Ask for feedback from those present using the feedback form below. Written feedback is better than oral feedback because you can take it away and reflect on it. Oral feedback works well between equals who have developed a very open relationship, but unfortunately this is not the norm in most organizations. Some of the usual problems with face to face feedback are as follows:

- People normally feel the need to be kind in a face to face encounter, so the feedback is less honest.
- In a face to face encounter you will react instinctively against any negatives by feeling depressed, embarrassed or making excuses for your performance. If the feedback is written, you can look at it several times, which helps you to form a more rational, positive approach to improving your skills.

Facilitation skills feedback form

Facilitator _____

Observer _____

Date _____

Area of competence   Comments   Score out of 5
1 = very poor, 3 = satisfactory, 5 = excellent

Pre-workshop planning
Was the agenda clear? Did you get enough warning? Did you get enough pre-workshop information?

Introduction to the workshop
Did the facilitator introduce the topic clearly? Were the workshop ground rules made clear at the start?

Keeping people involved
Was everyone actively encouraged to take part?

Managing time
Did the workshop end on time? Was all the ground covered adequately?

Making things clear
Did the facilitator encourage participants to clarify their contributions? Did anyone get lost along the way?

Managing discussion
Did all participants have sufficient airtime? Was the discussion guided, or did it go off track?

The next steps
Did the facilitator explain what happens now that the workshop is over?

Any other comments?

CHAPTER 8

Worked case studies

A man of words and not of deeds,
Is like a garden full of weeds.
English proverb

Theory without practice is of little use in business. Just as a man of words and not of deeds has his drawbacks, so too does a book on facilitation which does not feature any real examples of facilitated workshops in action. The four cases below tackle this issue by taking you through four actual workshops from instigation to the actions resulting.

These examples will help the reader to have a clearer picture of how facilitated workshops can be used to achieve organizational goals. The workshops described below are by no means perfect, but they all worked reasonably well. Some problems arose, and some parts could have been better. These areas are identified below, and are discussed as part of the full description of the workshop process.

Help-desk review workshop

Joe Green was pleased about his appointment as IT Manager in the software department of an insurance company. However, after a few weeks of doing the job, he became concerned about the level of complaints he was receiving from his colleagues about the in-house system support help-desk.

The help-desk had been in operation for two years and appeared to consume a lot of effort. Three full time staff worked on the help-desk, and others were pulled in from the development team on an *ad hoc* and increasingly time-consuming basis. The atmosphere amongst the help-desk staff had become very tense as they felt overloaded and undervalued. They were also finding it increasingly difficult to persuade development staff to work on support problems.

Joe was an experienced facilitator, and decided that a facilitated workshop for users would not only help him to find out what was going wrong, but would also demonstrate to users that his department was listening and willing to act on advice. He also decided to send out a survey to gauge customer opinion, and he interviewed the help-desk staff and several of the development staff individually to get their views of the problem.

Defining the workshop purpose

Joe defined the workshop purpose as follows:

The help-desk review workshop is intended to provide a forum for users to give their views about the current quality of help provided by the in-house system support help-desk. Participants will also be asked to give their views about the quality of help that they will require in the short and long-term future. These views will be recorded and discussed with help-desk and development staff, with a view to making the necessary improvements in the help-desk provision.

Planning the workshop

Joe decided that the help-desk staff should not be present at the workshop, but should view the results in private after the workshop was over. He wanted to allow the users to be frank, and thought that the presence of help-desk staff at the meeting might be inhibiting and even confrontational.

Joe invited each of the six Business Managers to send two members of staff who regularly used the help-desk, encouraging them to send one Insurance Executive and one Office Administrator so that both roles were represented.

He settled on a half-day workshop, as he thought that the ground could be easily covered in half a day. No preparation material was sent out, but those attending were asked to think about what they really wanted from the in-house system support help-desk both now and in the future. They were also asked to think about how they rated the current performance of the help-desk.

The workshop plan was as below. Joe decided to use the results of the customer survey to add depth to the workshop. This survey was sent out to all 400 potential users, 50 per cent of whom replied. It simply asked each respondent to rate the help-desk on ten different criteria, and then pick the three most important criteria. The survey indicated that all ten criteria were of around equal importance, and that the help-desk was seriously under-performing on speed of response, technical know-how of staff and keeping people informed.

Help-desk Review Workshop

Wednesday 6 June
09.00–12.00
Agenda

You are invited to attend a help-desk review workshop. This workshop is intended to provide an opportunity for you to give your views about the current quality of help provided by the in-house system support help-desk. You will also be asked to give your views about the quality of help provided at present, and about the type of help you will require in the short- and long-term future. Please therefore spend some time thinking about current and future help-desk activities.

The views gathered will be recorded, and then discussed with help-desk and development staff, with a view to making the necessary improvements in the help-desk provision.

9.00	Welcome and introduction
9.15	Rating current performance
10.45	COFFEE
11.00	Looking ahead – future requirements
12.00	CLOSE

Help-desk Review Workshop

	Time and activity	Duration	Who
9.00	Welcome and introductions – Each person explains his/her role and how he/she currently uses the help-desk. Ground rules – aim for improvement, one person speaks at any one time, no firm decisions will be made (only recommendations).	15 mins	Full group

9.15	**Rating current performance – Ask participants to rate the help-desk using a pre-determined set of criteria. Recognize that participants are being asked to give their ratings again. Let them know that this is just to gauge views of those present, to see how representative the group is of the company as a whole.** **Gather participant ratings together and display to workshop. Discuss views represented – reasons for high scores, low scores, most important criteria, least important criteria. Examine survey results. Notice how they differ from the views of those present.**	45 mins	Full group
10.00	**Divide into small groups. Each group to come up with ten concrete things that could be done better by the help-desk staff.**	30 mins	Small groups
10.30	**Gather a full list of strengths and areas for improvement – extracting overlaps. Ask for votes in the full group to find out which of these are the most important.**	15 mins	Full group
10.45	**COFFEE**		
11.00	**Looking further ahead – Split the group into pairs. Each pair should represent a section of the business. Ask each pair to think about the future demands on the help-desk from their section of the business in terms of increase in number of users, changes in ways of working, different systems, etc. Ask each pair to star (**) any especially important areas.**	20 mins	Pairs
11.20	**Ask each pair to present the changes predicted from their area.** **Generate a resulting list of 'areas to think about for the future' for the help-desk staff.**	40 mins	Full group
12.00	**CLOSE**		

Running the workshop

The workshop ran to time, covering the ground required. Some participants complained when they had to fill the survey in a second time, but understood the need for this as the workshop progressed. Two of the Insurance Executives thought that the ground covered in the first hour or so was a bit repetitive, but the others disagreed. Over half of the Office Administrators present did not really understand what was wanted from the discussion about the future. They left the thinking and talking up to the Insurance Executives. Joe thought that this problem could have been avoided if he had asked the Business Managers to brief the participants on future requirements before the workshop.

Following up afterwards

After the workshop, Joe produced a report detailing the full survey results, the group's survey results and the views of the group on the necessary short-term improvements and the requirements for the future. This was circulated to all those who came to the workshop, plus all Business Managers, the Chief Executive and the Finance Director. The last two recipients were given copies to encourage them to give their support to any requests for resources resulting from this exercise.

Joe then met with the help-desk staff to discuss the full set of results. Several decisions were then made, in consultation with development staff and senior managers. A memo was subsequently sent out to all staff detailing a programme of change for the help-desk. This included details concerning changes in personnel, planned training programmes, the introduction of a new system for tracking calls and the provision of better on-line facilities for help-desk staff.

Standards and procedures workshop

Sue was the manager of the Organizational Consultancy arm of a training company. This part of the company was beginning to grow, but had never set out any fundamental standards and procedures. Work was being done to the standards set out in the training manual, but these were only meant to cover training handouts and overheads. Staff and clients were starting to complain about this state of affairs. The staff wanted a clear format to work to, and the clients wanted the consultants to be consistent. Sue also thought it was important for all clients to receive the same level of service.

Sue decided to run a workshop to help formulate a set of standards and procedures for producing consultancy documents such as reports, presentations and handouts, project plans, letters, faxes, proposals and e-mails.

Sue was a fairly experienced facilitator, but had never had to produce standards or procedures before. As part of her research into this area, Sue visited a management consultancy which was being run to strict standards and procedures. This gave her some ideas as to how to direct the workshop, which she decided to run herself.

Defining the workshop purpose

Sue defined the workshop purpose as follows:

> *The standards and procedures workshop is intended to help the consultancy group to gather ideas for establishing ways of producing, reviewing and setting out documents. After the workshop, a draft set of standards and procedures will be written by Tom Brett. The group will meet again to review his first draft.*

Planning the workshop

Sue decided to invite all six consultants, as she wanted to involve people as much as possible from the start. This included Tom who was relatively new to the consultancy arena. She hoped that this involvement would get people interested and committed. She also hoped that it would help Tom to tap into the knowledge of the more experienced consultants.

Sue chose to make this workshop a one-day event. She wanted to make it enjoyable and creative, and also to help with team building because the consultants rarely had the time to get together.

The agenda and workshop design both appear below:

Standards and Procedures Workshop

Thursday 16 September
09.30–17.00
Agenda

Owing to several recent staff and client comments, I think it is a good time for us to get together to discuss standards and procedures for document production in the consultancy group. You are therefore asked to attend the above workshop.

The standards and procedures workshop is intended to help us to gather ideas for establishing ways of producing, reviewing and setting out documents. After the workshop, a draft set of standards and procedures will be written by Tom Brett. The group will meet again to review his first draft. Please make a big effort to come to the workshop. If you cannot come for any reason, let me know well in advance because we may be able to change the date.

Please have a think about how you produce your various documents at present, what is good about this process and what could be improved. Please also think about any standard document formats that you would recommend.

Agenda for the day:

9.30	Introduction
	Different types of document
	What constitutes a good document?
	What we do well and what could be improved
11.00	COFFEE
	Ten rules for setting out documents
12.45	LUNCH
14.00	Video and discussion of possible pitfalls of implementing standards and procedures
15.00	TEA
15.20	Developing procedures for numbering, reviewing, signing off and recording documents.
	Round up and evaluation
17.00	CLOSE

Standards and Procedures Workshop Design

	Time and activity	Duration	Who?
9.30	Introduction. Which cartoon character do you most closely resemble when you are carrying out your consultancy work? Agree ground rules. Present reasons for workshop, and findings from visit to management consultancy.	30 mins	Full group
10.00	Quick brainstorm to generate a list of different types of documents produced by the consultancy. Categorize the list into broader types of documents.	15 mins	Full group
10.15	Ask the group to work in pairs. Get them to think about real examples of each type of document – one good and one bad, and to conclude for each type what constitutes a good document (list at least five relevant characteristics for each type).	15 mins	Pairs
10.30	Gather these ideas on the flipchart, asking each pair for a contribution in turn. For each broad type of document, gather ideas on what is currently done well within the consultancy and what could be improved, using examples and focusing on business needs. Use a balance sheet flipchart for each type.	10 mins	Full group
	Pin these up around the room.	20 mins	Full group
11.00	COFFEE		
11.20	Split into two groups. Each group is asked to come up with a rough list of ten standard, practical rules for setting out an effective document of each type. The groups are asked to incorporate the comments gathered earlier. Each group prepares to present these to the other group, justifying the choice of rules.	40 mins	Threes

	Presentations. Groups present their findings and agree a full set of recommended rules for Tom to take away.	45 mins	Full group
12.45	LUNCH		
14.00	Video. Show entertaining and amusing video from the consultancy library illustrating the pitfalls of developing and implementing procedures and standards.	30 mins	Full group
14.30	Discuss potential pitfalls of this process, and think of ways of minimizing these problems. Use a spider diagram to capture the pitfalls, drawing circles around the key pitfalls. Draw lines out of each bubble to represent the possible ways of minimizing each problem.	30 mins	Full group
15.00	TEA		
15.20	Look at procedures for numbering, reviewing, signing off and keeping records of documents. Split the group into threes (different people this time). Give each group a long piece of paper (three pieces of flipchart paper stuck together). Get them to draw out the life of a document of each different type, including how it is allocated a number, how it is reviewed, by whom, who signs it off and how copies are kept. Explain use of boxes, diamonds and lines to represent activities, decisions and flow.	40 mins	Threes
16.00	Pin the resulting diagrams up on the walls and ask the groups to talk them through. Each participant then distributes five stars indicating an item which is particularly strong or necessary. Similarly, each participant is asked to stick up five red blobs. Each one indicates an item which the participant believes to be unnecessary or a weak idea.	40 mins	Full group
	Final roundup and evaluation of the workshop – did we achieve our aim?	20 mins	Full group
17.00	CLOSE		

115

Running the workshop

The workshop ran well. There was some confusion about the differences between standards and procedures. Some participants found the divide artificial at first, but most thought it a useful way of distinguishing between layout and document management. There was a lot of fruitful constructive discussion, which resulted in a great deal of ground being covered. The workshop ran to schedule.

Following up afterwards

Tom wrote up a workshop report which represented all the views generated. He explained in the report that he could not incorporate everyone's views as some of them were contradictory, but that he would make sensible compromises and try to include as many of the key requirements as possible.

Tom developed a draft set of procedures and standards, and the group met again six weeks later. The group were very pleased with the contents, and were able to recognize their own contributions. A few changes were made, but the draft was basically accepted. When the standards and procedures became the policy of the group, they were adopted with ease.

IT strategy workshop for senior managers

Natasha was a Senior Consultant working for a management consultancy, specializing in IT strategies. She was working on a project for a hospital in the UK.

The hospital was using a variety of IT systems for tasks such as administering outpatients, running the wards, monitoring finance and running the pharmacy. None of these systems could 'speak' to each other, resulting in many instances where data entered in one system had to be re-entered by hand into another system. The hospital wanted Natasha to examine all their existing IT systems, and produce a report recommending how they might proceed towards their goal of having a coherent set of integrated systems.

Natasha examined the systems and interviewed staff about the effectiveness of these systems. She then constructed a system model around which a coherent set of IT systems could be based and developed a set of four different strategies which the hospital could pursue to develop a fully integrated IT solution. These strategies were planned out, given a timescale and costed. Natasha then produced a report summarizing her findings and suggestions. She then planned to hold a workshop for senior managers to enable them to decide which of the four different strategies to follow.

Defining the workshop purpose

Natasha defined the purpose of the workshop as follows:

The purpose of the workshop is to involve the hospital senior managers in deciding which one of the four suggested strategies to use to achieve the proposed system model. The final decision will be taken by the Chief Executive together with the Finance Director, using the recommendations of this workshop.

Planning the workshop

Natasha decided to run a half-day workshop addressing the above issue. The Chief Executive together with Natasha identified who should attend. They needed to invite all the senior managers whose commitment was necessary to achieve the introduction of the new systems. The participants were Chief Executives, IT Managers, Finance Director, Quality Director, three Clinical Directors and Personnel Director. Natasha circulated her report two weeks before the workshop, with this agenda attached.

Running the workshop

The workshop was lively and purposeful. Most participants admitted that they had only skimmed through the report because they thought all would become clear at the workshop. They appreciated the chance to ask and be asked questions about the system model, which everyone except the IT Manager struggled with initially.

Natasha had to manage the presentations quite closely. This was because the participants began to stray away from talking about the basic elements of each strategy and on to talking about the pros and cons of each strategy before they had fully grasped the details.

The balance sheet approach was very much enjoyed by all, and everyone contributed freely. The final choice decided openly via the balance sheet scores was the same as the choice selected by secret voting.

IT Strategy Workshop for Senior Managers

15 March
09.30–13.00
Agenda

You are invited to attend a senior management workshop, at which you will be asked for your views about which of four proposed strategies the hospital should pursue in order to progress towards a coherent, integrated set of IT systems.

I attach my report which evaluates your existing IT set-up, recommends a new system model and proposes four different ways in which you can progress towards a coherent set of integrated systems.

Please read the report, paying special attention to the new system model. It is essential that you understand this model before you decide how the hospital should progress. Bring along any questions that you have about the model, and we will begin the workshop by addressing these. Please also study the four proposed strategies. These are planned out and costed in the report.

Agenda for the day:

9.30	Introduction
	Understanding the proposed system model
	Becoming familiar with the four different strategies for progress
11.00	COFFEE
11.15	Examining the different strategies – pros and cons of each
	Making a recommendation re the 'best fit' strategy
13.00	CLOSE

IT Strategy Workshop for Senior Managers
Workshop Design

	Time and activity	Duration	Who
9.30	Introduction – explain the purpose of the workshop, and the agenda for the morning. Ask each person to tell you if he or she has read the report, and if so to tell you: ● One thing in the report that confirmed something he or she already knew ● One thing in the report that was surprising	15 mins	Full group
9.45	Present the model briefly and ask for questions from the group. Use own pre-prepared quiz if no questions are forthcoming. Ask each person to complete the quiz. Discuss answers in full group.	45 mins	Full group
10.30	Split the group into pairs. Ask each pair to examine one of the four strategies for implementation. Ask them to prepare a five-minute presentation for the others in the group based on reading the report. The presentation should highlight the key elements of this strategy, set out its cost and time implications, and identify any parts of the strategy which are not clear.	30 mins	Pairs
11.00	COFFEE		
11.15	Participants give short presentations. Discussion of four proposed strategies.	30 mins	Full group
11.45	Use one balance sheet per strategy, and get the group to list the pros and cons of each, keeping all four sheets visible. Give each pro and con a score out of ten by agreement with the group. Add the pro scores and subtract the con scores to see which strategy scores the highest.	60 mins	Full group

> **Do a final secret vote to see which
> strategy the group recommends.**
> 12.45   **Recap and summarize.**   **Full group**
> 13.00   **CLOSE**

Following up afterwards

Natasha wrote a report summarizing what happened at the workshop, especially detailing the pros and cons listed for each strategy, together with their scores. This report was circulated widely throughout the organization, so that everyone was kept informed of progress. The Chief Executive was pleased with the work done, and used the report to make the decision as to how to progress. Further workshops were held later in the process to help people to prepare for implementation of new systems.

Prototype review workshop

Jim worked for a software company specializing in building systems for clients in the insurance and banking sector. Jim was leading the development of a system to record and search through a very large set of insurance policies. Because the client was not quite sure exactly what he wanted, the initial part of the project was being done on a time hire basis, until the client settled on a firm specification for the user interface. A time hire contract means that all work done by the supplier is paid for by the client on a daily rate basis.

Jim and his team had built a prototype system based on initial sketchy requirements which was intended to act as a starting point for discussion. Jim decided to run a half-day workshop for the client users to demonstrate the prototype and to encourage them to make comments about its suitability.

Defining the workshop purpose

The workshop purpose was defined as follows:

> *The prototype review workshop aims to demonstrate the current user interface prototype to a group of users who can constructively comment on its suitability. The comments will all be recorded, and the Project Board will*

120

then use these comments to enable them to decide at the next Project Board meeting which changes should be incorporated and which should not.

Planning the workshop

Jim was an experienced software engineer, so he knew that a prototype review workshop had to be carefully planned and introduced. He needed to ensure that the workshop did not raise unrealistic user expectations of either what could actually be achieved with the available technology or what could be changed within the prevailing cost and timescale boundaries.

Jim invited the four client Business Managers and the Project Sponsor. He also suggested that each Business Manager should bring along an experienced user of the current system. The experienced users could then give in-depth knowledge of the typical functions carried out regularly.

Jim decided to set up the demonstration so that each group of three participants would be able to view a screen. He set up a PC with three 'slave' terminals. He decided to run the demo himself on the PC (the system was not in a state to be 'played' with by users, as it was only a prototype) and each group of three participants would sit in front of a slave terminal to watch the demo. He decided to ask two members of his development team to attend to answer technical questions, so that he could concentrate on facilitating. Jim nominated himself as scribe.

Jim's memo inviting participants to the Prototype Review Workshop is shown below.

Prototype Review Workshop

12th October
09.00–12.00
Agenda

Please attend a half-day workshop to review the user interface prototype for the DREX system. We have built a prototype according to the initial broad specifications, and now we would like you to give us some feedback on how appropriate it is to your needs.
I attach a copy of the initial broad guidelines, which were agreed in June. These initial requirements are fixed, but any changes outside of this will be noted and put forward for approval by your Project Board.
Agenda for the day:

9.00	Introduction
	Capabilities of the chosen technology
	Recap of cost and timescale parameters
	Demonstration of system
10.30	COFFEE
10.45	Discussion of feedback
	Voting on most important and least important areas
12.30	CLOSE

The workshop design appears below:

Prototype Review Workshop Design

	Time and activity	Duration	Who
9.00	Introduction. Ask each person to say which two elements of the old system they would like to keep, and what two developments they would like to see in the new system. Restate the firm nature of requirements agreed so far. Explain the capabilities of the chosen technology – what can be done and what cannot be done. Recap on cost and timescale	30 mins	Full group
9.30	parameters. Demonstrate system. Ask participants to watch each section of the demo before asking questions. Each section of the demo is five minutes long, four sections in total. Encourage participants to make notes on the strengths and weaknesses of each section under the following headings:	60 mins	Full group (working in threes)

- the functionality of the system
- the navigation between different screens and menus
- the general look and feel of the system

	Take questions after each section, but ask participants to save all feedback until after coffee.		
10.30	COFFEE		
10.45	Discuss feedback one section at a time. Use a balance chart to record strengths and weaknesses for each section.	75 mins	Full group
	Ask each participant to indicate which weaknesses are most serious by distributing 15 ticks across all the weaknesses identified. Participants each place their ticks directly on the flipchart lists – set a maximum of three ticks per person per item. Add up the ticks for each weakness.	10 mins	Individual
	Recap and summarize.	20 mins	Full group
12.30	CLOSE		

Running the workshop

The workshop was stimulating and purposeful. It ran over time by half an hour because one particular area of functionality seemed to be causing a lot of problems and needed extra discussion. Jim negotiated an extension of the timing with the group.

The group liked the structure and involvement, and particularly appreciated the drawing of boundaries at the start, which meant that they did not waste time asking for things which could not be delivered.

One participant did not contribute very much for the first half of the workshop. Jim asked him about this privately during the break, and discovered that he did not use the computer system regularly enough to have a view. His boss had asked him to come just to get him involved.

Jim found it quite difficult to facilitate and scribe at the same time, especially during the question and answer sessions. On reflection, he would rather have had another team member present to act as scribe.

Following up afterwards

Jim wrote a report listing the questions asked by participants and the responses given by technical staff, plus the strengths and weaknesses identified by the group. The tick scores were also recorded. Jim also added some information about how long each change would take to implement, and how much it would cost.

The Project Board was impressed with the constructive nature of the list of possible changes, and found the scores particularly useful. This helped them to sift through the list and identify the priorities.

CHAPTER 9

Special case workshops

What is a special case workshop?

Of course, every workshop is a special case. There is no such thing as a standard, repeatable workshop. Three factors are at play here:

- Each group you work with as a facilitator has a different dynamic because of the unique mix of people present, so you have to be able to react using a range of techniques and styles.
- The issues for an organization or team will change in shape and importance over time, so you will be tackling these in a range of ways as time moves on.
- Different people will perceive the issues differently so their reactions, energy level and amount of creativity will vary considerably.

There are two types of workshop event that do deserve special attention in this book, because in these two cases there is more to think about, more at stake and more that can go wrong! I have chosen top team workshops and cross-cultural workshops, because I believe that these are the two areas where there is most leverage to be gained from good preparation.

In this section I am particularly indebted to my trusted colleagues and good friends Alex Clark and Anne-Marie Saunders of Relay Consultants. Alex and Anne-Marie spent some time with me sharing their reflections on their facilitation work with a wide variety of cross-cultural groups of senior managers from organizations such as Hewlett Packard and STMicroelectronics.

Top team workshops

Question: When is a team not a team?

Answer: When it's a top team!

It's a cheap joke, and not always true. Nonetheless, there is a nugget to hold on to here. Top teams comprise bright, successful, highly competent people with strong agendas. The senior team members are usually measured on the performance of their own function, so their agendas often conflict. The top team in an organization probably does not spend a lot of time together as a team. So the picture of an effective working team might not be accurate.

What do I mean by a top team workshop? A top team workshop involves the most senior managers in an organization sitting down together, creating a shared understanding of an issue and working towards decisions and action. Examples include:

- creating a product strategy;
- looking at cultural change;
- considering structural change;
- planning for a merger;
- developing cross-functional working.

A facilitator might be requested for a top team workshop in the hope that this will provide:

- stimulation and interest;
- outside knowledge;
- a process;
- someone to organize their thinking;
- a catalyst for action;
- team behaviour feedback;
- an arbitrator (less often);
- a scapegoat if it all goes wrong (careful – it can happen!).

You need to be sure why the top team wants a facilitator, what they expect from you, who they have used before and how well that worked. Facilitation means different things to different people. This can range from making a major content pitch through to managing discussion through to observing and feeding back at the end. You can be sure that a top team will have high standards and clear expectations, so get your role crystal clear before you start.

Preparation is critical

Preparation is critical with a top team workshop. You need at least twice your normal amount of preparation so that you appear credible and so that your agenda and structure focuses on their key issues. Buy-in to the workshop is important, and this is best gained by one to one conversations with each participant before the event.

- Arrange one-to-one conversations with as many participants as possible. This allows you to check out each person's agenda and to set some expectations for them. (Persevere in tracking people down and getting them to return your calls. Try e-mail as well as telephone if necessary. Ensure that the benefits to *them* of this conversation with you are clear.)
- Read relevant company documents so that you are completely up to date on the current issues (not just the one you are dealing with in the workshop).
- Prepare your opening pitch, including relevant groundrules, very carefully.
- Find out what workshops have been held before and how they went.
- Find out as much as you can about the participants (roles, history, future, key relationships, expertise).

Be wise about behaviour

Senior people can become very good at demonstrating behavioural agreement. This means they look as if they agree and have bought in, but they fail to take the necessary action. Be aware that this can happen in top team workshops. If senior managers find that behavioural agreement works effectively for them, they will use it habitually. If you hold one-to-one sessions with each senior manager before the workshop, this behaviour is much less likely to happen, as they will have already shared some of their real thoughts with you. Your job will be to enable the group to raise important issues openly and constructively and to ensure that agreed actions are followed up.

Senior groups of men can be quite brutal with each other, and potentially with you, the facilitator. This comes with the territory to some extent, so if you are faint-hearted then stand well back! The senior managers are pretty tough (usually) so do not be over alarmed on their account. Stick to your principles of encouraging everyone to share their views and of keeping to the relevant issues.

Be aware of the power in the room. You are not totally free to quieten people down. For instance, lower status top team members will stay quiet once asked to be quiet. They might get back at you for this later outside the workshop. Higher status top team members will naturally resist attempts to shut them off. It is wise to check up-front with team members how they would like you to act if you think they have gone on for too long.

If you are well prepared, you should be able to ride any criticism during the workshop of your own performance pretty well. Don't respond directly – it's best to revisit the groundrules and to reiterate the goals of the workshop. Usually the criticism says more about their own frustrations than it does about your performance.

Know what you bring

Senior managers bring a lot of expertise and experience. They will challenge you and expect you to be expert and experienced in your own area. This means that your credibility is important and needs to be established early on. Let them know what you bring to the workshop in terms of relevant skills, experience and knowledge and do this early on.

Don't expect your sponsor to know everything and do everything

Who is your contact point? Your workshop sponsor might or might not be one of the top team. Either way, he or she will have a unique view of the issues. Don't expect his or her perceptions to be 'the truth'. Before the workshop, check your sponsor's view by talking to others (especially about the main issues) to ensure you gather different readings. Also be aware of how powerful and well respected your sponsor is. This will give you a filter to use on sponsor-supplied information and may help you to understand who you have to build relationships with to make the workshop credible and effective.

If your sponsor is efficient, well respected and communicative, then you are unlikely to encounter problems with arrangements and expectation management. However, you might not be so lucky. At top team level, it is better to make sure things are done than to make a false assumption. Make a checklist of all the things that need to be arranged (equipment, hotels, refreshments, message passing, e-mail access etc) and communicated (informing participants, sending out pre-reading, identifying workshop aims, setting date and time, informing other key stakeholders). Follow this through with your sponsor and the relevant administrative staff.

Beware diversions into detail

Top teams have a tendency to drop down into discussion of tactical and operational issues because it's easier, safer and more immediate. The bigger strategic issues are harder to grasp and the solutions are less obvious. A carefully applied ground rule will help here, but the facilitator needs to be aware when this type of diversion is happening, and not be put off by the amount of interest generated by a simple operational problem. Hand signals can help to indicate the need to come up a level; better than a verbal rebuke. Use a palm up gesture to encourage participants to get out of the detail.

Keep it snappy and keep them involved

Top teams need to be quickly engaged in a topic and involved early. Keep your inputs short (20 minutes maximum) and make sure discussions are well structured. Top teams need to be sure they are heading for concrete action – don't take too long getting there.

Cross-cultural workshops

You like potato, and I like potahto. You like tomato, and I like tomahto; Potato, potahto, tomato, tomahto! Let's call the whole thing off!

But oh! If we call the whole thing off, then we must part.
And oh! If we ever part, then that might break my heart!

So if you like pajamas and I like pajahmas, I'll wear pajamas and give up pajahmas.
For we know we need each other, so we'd better call the calling off off.
Fred Astaire and Ginger Rogers in the film *Shall We Dance*
Words by Ira Gershwin, music by George Gershwin.

The famous Gershwin song is well loved and much repeated. It also contains a neat analogy for us as cross-cultural facilitators. The couple in the song are obviously in love but are threatening to call off a relationship because of language differences. They see sense before the end of the song, and I suspect that if they stick at this thing, they will have a fruitful, loving and exciting relationship! Variety is the spice of life. We need difference of every sort to gain new perspectives and new learning in any context, and we need to work at working together.

So what do we mean in this book by cross-cultural? In a sense, every workshop is cross-cultural. There is always difference within the backgrounds of any group of workshop participants in at least three of four of the categories listed below:

- knowledge;
- skills;
- age;
- years of service with the organization;
- management level;
- education;
- nationality;
- gender;
- ethnic origin;
- first language;
- experience;
- physical ability;
- functional perspective (eg marketing, operations, HR);
- intelligence;
- drive;
- personality type.

Traditionally, the term 'cross-cultural' means cross-national. I choose to widen the definition out to include cross-functional and cross-organizational. This will help us to explore the general topic of facilitating diverse groups, but also emphasises the necessity to look beyond the obvious national differences ('the British are reserved', 'the French are expressive' etc).

These glaring national differences are interesting and can sometimes be informative (see Geert Hofstede's (1996) *Cultures and Organizations* if you have a real need to get into the details of cultural difference at a national level). However, I would treat these differences as something to be aware of, rather than as a starting point for second guessing the real issues. In the worst case, discussion of these national differences will descend into excuses for maintaining opposed views and creating a feeling of superiority.

Two rules should be used as guidance when running diverse workshops:

Rule 1: The more complex the mix, the more careful you need to be and the more planning you need to do.

Rule 2: Believe it can be done! Mixed groups can achieve a shared understanding of the key issues and can move together towards decisions and action.

I have split the topic of facilitating mixed groups into several headings, which capture the points worth considering.

Clarity of purpose

The purpose needs to be absolutely clear for any workshop, but especially for a diverse group. Try to use simple language. Avoid business jargon and slang expressions when facilitating for a group with diverse ability in the language being used.

Spend at least 20 minutes at the start of the workshop explaining what is going to happen. Give people who have come a long way a chance to arrive both physically and psychologically. Give people of differing management levels some reassurance that they will not be exposed.

It is important to set ground rules. Try to anticipate any practical problems that might occur and use ground rules at the start of the workshop to enlist the help of the group. For instance, if you are bringing together Marketing and Operations people who have traditionally struggled to talk constructively with each other, you might anticipate problems with listening. In this case you would emphasize the purpose of the workshop ie to create a shared view and increase understanding of other perspectives, and set a ground rule which enlists the help of participants in ensuring that everyone listens and everyone has their say. You can monitor this as you go along.

Activity type

Mixed groups need a mix of activities. For instance finance, accounting or computing staff might be more naturally reflective and sales staff more naturally active. Make sure that there is time for reflection and time for action to accommodate this potential difference.

Be aware that different nationalities place a greater or lesser importance on status and seniority. Whereas it would be quite acceptable in the Netherlands or the United Kingdom to ask a competent junior person to lead a small group discussion, or to expect the more junior staff to voice their opinions in open forum, this would be likely to be less comfortable for anyone from South East Asia. Construct your activities accordingly, ensuring that everyone feels comfortable to give a view.

Check out how comfortable the participants are with the workshop format. My experience is that French participants are more used to didactic training scenarios, and need encouragement to participate freely (do not take this as fact!). You would need to break participants in gently and keep a close watch on small group work.

Some US participants, especially on the West Coast might have been to some fairly wacky events and might be expecting more variety and sheer entertainment than you have bargained for! This might also be true for any large, multi-national company in the United Kingdom. Check this out with colleagues and contacts, and plan your activities accordingly. What are they expecting? Can you deliver?

My experience in the United Kingdom with public sector organizations is that they might have sat through several fairly similar workshops: sometimes excellent and sometimes to no avail. This means you have to be quite original in how you tackle issues to make an impact.

Use of images and metaphors

A client told me recently of a difficulty he encountered at a cross-national senior management workshop he attended. The large multinational electronics company for whom he works as Regional HR Manager was tackling the issue of changing job roles. The UK-based consultants facilitating the event brought the Charles Handy *inverted doughnut* model with them to explore this topic and stimulate discussion.

The inverted doughnut model uses the American definition of a ring doughnut with a hole in the middle. Handy inverts the doughnut to illustrate the modern job: filled in the centre (core job), and with a hole on the outside (room to grow, learn and be flexible).

This would have been an excellent model, except that a full hour was taken up with confusion amongst the French, North American, British and Italian as to what exactly a doughnut was. In America it's a ring with a hole in the middle. In France, there is no such thing. Was this a bagel? The Italians were lost. In the United Kingdom a doughnut has jam instead of a hole. How do you invert the jam? Even the Regional HR Manager, a Brit, came back having missed the point completely.

Images and metaphors need to be chosen very carefully for cross-cultural groups. They can so easily become confusing and unhelpful. Images using nature are very strong, as everyone will understand these readily. Talk of challenges such as climbing mountains, journeys along a fast flowing river and crossing rough seas will create shared meaning quickly.

Use of examples

In some workshops, the facilitator will need to give examples to illustrate a new way of thinking, or to identify the type of results required from an activity or to inform people about how other units/organizations tackle a particular issue.

Examples should be chosen with care for diverse groups. Make sure that examples are drawn from as many relevant sources as possible (different functional areas, different types of organization, different cultural background, different gender/ethnic type). This ensures that all participants feel equally valued and included, so will therefore contribute equally.

Use of language

If the workshop is being run in a language other than the first language of all participants then make sure you get familiar with each individual's command of the language being used. I sometimes pair non-fluent people with an appropriate co-participant and ask them to spend a little time together in the breaks discussing what went on, and making sure the person follows the flow of the workshop.

As the facilitator you need to use clear, simple language. Use pictures and natural metaphors (see above) as much as possible to develop quick shared understanding of issues being tackled.

Beware the nationality scapegoat

Many organizations now work across national boundaries as a matter of course, often without regular face-to-face contact and sometimes surviving only on e-mail contact. In many cases this all goes swimmingly as long as everyone has an agreed agenda and no major mistakes are made.

Workshop facilitators are often brought in when things go wrong or when things are about to change. It's then your job to get them to talk together constructively.

National difference might be an issue, but in an organization with a strong international culture such as Hewlett Packard, the differences between people more often arise from different functional perspectives, differing agendas or simply not knowing each other that well. So beware the instinct to put problems down to national or cultural difference.

I facilitated for a company recently where one flight of stairs separated two fairly similar groups of UK based teams more effectively than 20,000 miles of airspace!

Hosting

It is important to consider how best to *host* an event for people who have travelled a long way. This is especially important if any participant is visiting the country, area or organization for the first time. Hosting is not just about getting the coffee ready and the air conditioning right. Although it might not officially be your job as facilitator to organize the details of the event, your client or sponsor might need some help from you in making the event run smoothly and making it memorable. Here's a useful list of prompts:

● Is there time for people to check-in and check-out of the venue?
● When can visitors from other time zones pick up their e-mail or call home?
● West Coast USA people will expect breakfast to be part of the refreshment provision – what else will be expected in terms of refreshments? Apparently trivial cultural comforts go a long way towards making people feel comfortable.
● What time of day will visitors from other time zones be most alert? When I run workshops in the United States, the United Kingdom people are all up at 6am ready to go.

- If there is an overnight stay, is there something arranged for those who don't know the area? Advice on local restaurants or a provisional booking is useful.
- Do visitors want to see the local area, or visit the organization locally? It might be worthwhile to build this in.
- Have you considered providing the participants with a memento of the event, or area or the organization?

Choice of facilitator

Which cultural group do you represent? Be very conscious of who you might be seen to be representing as unnecessary tensions or barriers can be unwittingly set up if you get this dynamic wrong. Are you seen to be representing:

- Head office?
- Senior management?
- HR department?
- The old school?
- The new blood?
- The UK perspective?

It can be useful to *co-facilitate* to address the problems associated with this such as stereotyping, interpreting, cynicism and general defensiveness. Co-facilitating involves running the workshop with another facilitator, handing the reins over to each other for sections of the day. For instance, I co-facilitated a series of workshops on Process Improvement together with the company's Director of Quality. I represented HR and the development angle. He represented the company's commitment to quality and a process-driven approach. Those attending therefore understood that this was a company-wide initiative supported by training, rather than a didactic QA programme or an HR-led 'happy pill'.

To give another example, I co-facilitated an international workshop that brought a large group of marketing and IT design people together. I have IT design experience and my colleague brought the marketing perspective. What we hadn't thought about was the practicality of two '40 something' females facilitating a 30 strong all-male group with an average age of 29 years. Within a couple of hours we had (completely unintentionally) become mother hens, and they had become naughty schoolboys. One Finnish participant accused us of coming across like twin Margaret Thatchers! In retrospect one male and one female facilitator would have worked better, but pre-thinking the issues that might arise would have helped us to set some groundrules for acting.

STOP AND THINK!

Question 1

The HR Director of a large UK-based telecommunications company wants you to run a two-day workshop for the Management Board. The Management Board comprises: Financial Director, Operations Director, Marketing Director, Commercial Director, Quality Director, HR Director. The topic is 'Our Values' and the purpose is to come up with an agreed set of values for the business. The HR Director tells you that the Operations Director tends to follow his own dubious set of values instead of sticking to the company values. How would you tackle this?

Question 2

You are asked to facilitate a workshop that will bring together all 16 members of a marketing team. The purpose of the workshop is to help them to identify their work priorities and to create a high level plan for the coming two years.

Eight members of the team are French working out of Paris and the other 12 are British working out of Manchester. The team met as one group one year ago, but just for a brief chat. Since then one or two people have travelled both ways to solve specific technical issues. All other contact has been by telephone or e-mail.

The UK based Team Manager has asked you to facilitate as he is an old colleague of yours. He has expressed a desire to 'bring the French into alignment' via this workshop. He sees them as uncooperative and rather unpredictable. How would you respond?

CHAPTER 10

Facilitating virtual meetings

Yesterday upon the stair I met a man who wasn't there. He wasn't there again today. I wish that man would go away.
Hughes Mearns (1875–1965)

Virtual teams – how do they work?

Many teams in the organizations that I work with are *virtual*. Team members don't sit together in one room, or even along the same corridor. They tend to rely on technology to enable communication and collaboration. They may not all be working to a clear set of common objectives. Team members are often scattered across different sites, or even across the globe, operating in different environments for different local bosses and in different time zones. The team may have fluid membership with team members coming and going without the knowledge of the full team. There may be different national cultures represented on the team, with a number of native languages represented.

Life has become complicated for team leaders. The old theories about forming, storming, norming and performing do not apply for teams like this. The ideal situation of a static team in a single office focusing on neatly defined work packages is less and less common.

There are various types of virtual team. Here are the four that are most prevalent in today's organizations:

● *Network* – A network is a group of people who exchange information, knowledge and possibly resources. They may be asked to critique the work of others, gather research ideas or make proposals. The membership is fluid but the sense of purpose is clear. There are common interests. This type of group may cross organizational boundaries such as a network of IT providers and their suppliers.

- *Project group* – A project group is a fluid group of people with a defined output to be delivered in a specific timescale. The team has to complete work packages and make decisions together.
- *Production group* – A production group is a fixed team of people who perform regular ongoing work. Intranet software allows them to work on processes in an interconnected way across the organization. Finance, training and IT teams may work in this way.
- *Management team* – Management teams of global organizations often have to operate as virtual teams, relying on audio conferences or video conferences to communicate on a daily basis.

Although technology is a fundamental aspect of successful virtual team-working, there are other important factors that need to be attended to. Here is our top ten list of success criteria for a virtual team:

- *Team members are rewarded fairly and squarely on results* – rewards in virtual teams must not be made on the basis of familiarity, or personal presence, or any other criteria that rely on people meeting people every day at the water cooler.
- *Team members are offered training and coaching in use of relevant technology* – it's all very well to be given a pile of software to use, but how does it work, and what are the best ways of exploiting it? Other people's experiences and knowledge should be readily accessible.
- *Methods of working with other team members are agreed and well-known* – if my boss is in Mexico and I am in France, then what are the agreed ways in which we can work together? How and when do we discuss my performance? Is there a regular team briefing? If so, how is this done? What is my reporting mechanism?
- *There is equal access across the team to electronic communication and collaboration tools* – inequality in technology is an instant team-breaker. Make sure that everyone has access to the same tools.
- *The team operates in a high trust environment* – empowerment is the bedrock of virtual working, so people need to be competent and motivated, and therefore trusted, before they can work comfortably in a virtual environment. Competence comes when there is learning and development, and motivation comes from a match between the job itself and the individual's interests.

- *Leaders act as good role models for virtual teamworking* – leaders must respect the diversity of the team membership, and make a special effort to communicate evenly across the team.
- *Leaders set high expectations of the team* – virtual teams do not need virtual leaders. They need real leaders who can enthuse and engage people, even on the phone!
- *Leaders provide resources for team members to communicate and collaborate – both provision of necessary technology and of time and money to enable face to face meetings* – one manager described virtual working to me recently. 'It's like being pushed out into the middle of a huge lake in a boat with no oars.' Virtual working only delivers the goods when there are some easy, accessible ways of communicating and collaborating. Otherwise there will be unpleasant consequences such as duplicated work, unnecessary conflict, slow problem solving and a creative desert.
- *Team members are aware of the ground rules for working across boundaries* – ground rules are important to establish early on. Is it OK to miss a virtual team meeting? How long can you leave it before you need to reply to an e-mail from your colleagues in Japan? These questions need to be answered and ways of working embedded.
- *Team members are encouraged to take responsibility and make decisions where possible* – virtual teams can easily grind to a halt if there is too much red tape or too much unnecessary consultation and approval. These should be kept to a minimum.

Pros and cons of a virtual meeting

Virtual teams need to get together to discuss issues as all teams do. The reasons for getting together are:

- to generate ideas;
- to gather information;
- to share views;
- to consider options;
- to make decisions;
- to create plans;
- to air and resolve conflict.

Virtual teams do not always have the option of a face to face meeting because of money and time restrictions. It is often much easier to arrange a virtual meeting than it is to arrange a face to face one which is reliant on transport, and takes so much longer to organize and run. A virtual meeting may involve anything from simply setting up an audio conference to the more complex use of real-time data conferencing with audio and video links, together with electronic chat and whiteboard facilities.

So what are the pros and cons of virtual meetings?

Virtual meetings are attractive because they are:

● cheaper to organize than face to face meetings;
● easy to schedule;
● relatively easy to chair;
● time efficient;
● very good for issues that require focus – no distractions.

The downsides of virtual meetings are:

● Conflict between team members is harder to deal with when people are not face to face.
● Brainstorming and creative discussions are more challenging unless the technology is very sophisticated.
● The interaction can be slow and laborious, so the meeting is less energizing.
● Technology teething troubles can take an inordinate amount of time to solve, especially if encountered during the meeting.
● It's possible for some people to fail to contribute, and for this to go unnoticed. We call these people 'lurkers'.
● It's difficult to gauge whether you really have agreement due to lack of non-verbal signs.

Virtual meeting technologies and their applications

At the time of writing, all of the options listed below are tried and tested, and readily available. Some are much cheaper than others. I am confident that cheaper, simpler options will soon become available as this is a field that is developing fairly rapidly.

Audio conference

An audio conference is the simplest form of virtual meeting. The only technology necessary is the telephone. This type of meeting is most useful when there is a specific purpose in mind such as reviewing a document, or finalizing the details of an event. Brainstorming or creative thinking is quite difficult to achieve because of the disconnected sensation of unnamed voices coming from a dark cave. This type of meeting is not useful when there are more than six or seven people attending.

Video conference

Video conferencing is widely used in many global organizations. The bandwidth of your communications link must be high to make this worth doing, otherwise an audio conference works just as well. Slow links are frustrating and distracting, making the bonus of seeing people almost worthless as you spend needless effort trying to puzzle out their jerky actions. This type of meeting is useful for reasonably straightforward option consideration and decision-making, provided materials are available beforehand. It is also useful for initial meetings as a 'get to know you', or for working out conflicts if a face to face session is out of the question.

Real-time data conferencing

Real-time data conferencing features an audio line plus desktop internet access. This type of meeting is typically an hour long and involves working together on a common task. People can speak or e-mail their contributions, including attachments, and those with the required authorization can edit documents that are visible to all those participating. This might mean for instance working on a PowerPoint presentation, or a simulated whiteboard drawing. Voting systems may also be a feature.

This type of meeting is good for discussing and agreeing concepts and setting broad goals, for collecting data and discussing patterns and possibilities. It is also good for sharing views and information, and for generating enthusiasm and interest on a topic. Decisions can also be reached if these are not too complex, and especially if these decisions involve the production of a document.

Non real-time data conferencing

This type of meeting runs over the period of a few days. People contribute to discussion threads and post documents of interest. This may be as simple as a bulletin board or a chat room, or it may have more advanced features such as access to documents stored by other teams and the ability to control versions of local documents.

This is useful for broad discussions of trends and themes and the generation of ideas and options. It is less useful for decision-making or prioritizing, or for planning and setting actions.

E-mail

E-mail is the most widely used method for teams to communicate with each other and think together. I think it is used far too often when a simple phone call would do the job much more effectively. It is quick, direct and easy to use, and offers time for the receiver to reflect before replying (sometimes neglected). Replying to a reply and so on produces an automatic record of the thread of a discussion at no extra cost, thus simulating one aspect of the more expensive software on the market.

E-mail is useful for generating ideas, sharing views and gathering information, although version control is usually an issue once files are attached with similar names. Decision making with a group is very difficult via e-mail – like herding cats. Someone will always misunderstand or fail to reply. Conflict can be easily aired by e-mail, and is often created unwittingly by e-mail messages, but resolution requires a different medium such as the good old-fashioned telephone.

Tips for facilitating a virtual meeting

Virtual meetings require a different type of facilitation depending on the technology employed to provide the communication and collaboration. Here are our facilitation tips, grouped by technology.

Audio conference and video conference
- Be clear about the purpose of the meeting and draft a tight agenda.
- Declare a start and finish time and stick to it.
- With video conferencing, ensure that the equipment is set up 30 minutes before the meeting is due to start, and is thoroughly tested.

- Restrict numbers to no more than eight people.
- Circulate relevant materials well before the session.
- Let people know who is facilitating.
- Stop people if they stray off the point.
- Ask people to announce themselves as they enter, contribute to, or leave the meeting.
- Give pace and energy to the meeting by summarizing progress, asking key questions and offering structure.
- Provide minutes soon after the meeting.

Real-time data conferencing

- Be clear about the purpose of the meeting and draft a tight agenda.
- Declare a start and finish time and stick to it.
- Ensure that relevant materials are posted for all to see before the meeting starts.
- Decide how the meeting will run and stick to the sequence.
- Decide which tools you will use for what purpose eg whiteboard, chat room.
- If you are producing a document together, decide who will edit the document during the meeting and if more than one person, in what sequence this will be done.
- If there is voting, agree when this will be done and whether or not it will be anonymous.
- If the topic is complex, then set up a chat room facility in the days preceding the meeting, with some specific discussion threads and the help of an experienced facilitator. The facilitator should guide discussion in the right direction and summarize the threads the day before the meeting is due to happen.

Non real-time data conferencing

- Set discussion threads carefully and ensure everyone who is participating knows the purpose of this activity.
- Facilitate the conversation as the discussion progresses by asking for clarity, making links, picking up significant points that were missed and summarizing agreement.
- Let participants know when the conference is over and how the comments have been used.

E-mail

- Be specific about the information desired.

- Use reply to record the thread of discussion.
- Keep the copies to four or five people maximum.
- Let everyone know when you have gathered enough information, and what the decision is.

Dos and don'ts for virtual team managers and team members

Here is a list of general dos and don'ts for team managers and team leaders in virtual teams.

Team managers

Do:

- Meet face to face at least every three months.
- Establish purpose and team goals face to face.
- Ensure that virtual meeting times are rotated to allow for different time zones.
- Hold one-to-ones as well as group sessions.
- Enable members of the team to work together, even if travelling is necessary.
- Be a strong facilitator of virtual meetings – probably stronger than usual.
- Respond to team members' e-mails and voicemails quickly – especially for those who are far away.
- Nip conflict in the bud and deal with it quickly.

Don't:

- Keep cancelling and rescheduling meetings.
- Give more early information to the local team.
- Deal with individual issues during a virtual meeting.

Team members

Do:

- Find out how to use the technologies available.
- Tell your manager what you are up to.

- Respond to e-mails and voicemails quickly.
- Ask for help if you need it.
- Make an effort to contribute to discussions.
- Make a conscious effort to involve team members in other locations in work that you are doing.
- Devote full attention to virtual team meetings.

Don't:
- Just communicate with your local colleagues.
- Give virtual team meetings a low priority.
- Fail to prepare for virtual team meetings.
- Wait for your manager to ask you for information.

CHAPTER 11

The facilitator's complete checklist

Too busy to read the book? Don't worry. The checklists below will help you to see what you've missed. Then you can read the relevant chapter if you need to.

Checklist 1: Questions to ask upfront

(See Chapters 1, 2 ,3, 7 and 9)

- Why is the workshop happening now?
- What else is going on for this group of people?
- What else has 'worked' in this organization or for this group?
- What is the purpose of the event?
- Are there any other purposes?
- What are the challenges for this group right now? (business issues, organizational issues, results issues, external environment issues).
- Who's in the group? (background – see cross-cultural difference list in Chapter 9).
- How well do group members know each other (how do they work together?)
- What are the important relationships within the group?
- Can all the purposes be met via this workshop?
- Is there any pre and post work to be done? (eg coaching, informing, teaching).
- How engaged are this group in the topic?

- Is the boss coming? (or equivalent).
- Who else should be there?
- Who else should know about the workshop?

Checklist 2: Questions to ask when designing the workshop

(See Chapters 1, 3 and 9)

- How many participants are there?
- What are their backgrounds/preferences/nationalities etc?
- How long have we got?
- What do people need to go away with?
- How familiar are people with this topic? Is there any updating to be done? How will this be done?
- What's the mix of management levels? Is this significant?
- How much small group/big group discussion should there be?
- How much time should be spent on getting to know each other?
- How much time should be spent on tackling tasks?
- How will you manage each section of the workshop – what tools and techniques will you use?
- What's the balance between reflection and activity? Is this appropriate?
- Does the workshop flow make sense?
- Is there a theme for the whole workshop event?
- Have you devised a method for capturing thoughts, ideas and actions?
- Is there enough diversity of activity to retain interest?
- Have you considered the cultural mix? (see Chapter 9)
- Is it a top team? If so, read Chapter 9. You might need to speak to all participants before the workshop.

Checklist 3: Questions to ask about the actual event

(See Chapters 4 and 5)

- Have you got enough space, paper, flipcharts, wall space, blu-tack, pens, break-out rooms, refreshments?
- Have you planned well to accommodate visitors from afar (eg check-in, jet lag, calling home)?
- Does everyone know where to come?
- Does everyone know the purpose and have access to pre-reading?
- Have you prepared a strong piece at the start to position the event?
- Are you the right facilitator? Are you seen as unbiased? Is this important?
- Do you have a plan of what you are doing broken down into 30–60 minute blocks?
- Is your mind clear of distractions?
- Is the seating right? Can you see everyone?
- Will you be able to manage the discussion alone? Maybe you need a co-facilitator?

Checklist 4: Questions to ask afterwards

(See Chapters 6 and 7)

- How memorable was the event?
- Did the event achieve its purpose(s)?
- Did everyone get included?
- What should go in your workshop report? Will anyone read it?
- What is the best way of dealing with recorded information on flipcharts and notes?
- Do you recommend any next steps from your own perspective?
- How well did you do your bit?
- Have **you** arranged to unwind in an appropriate way? Work-shops are exhausting for the facilitator!

Answers to questions

Introducing facilitation

Question 1

Workshop sponsors may hope to use the workshop format to persuade a group of people to follow a course of action or to hold a particular view. This is a manipulative approach which is unlikely to work and may end up by aggravating the participants, especially when the participants are experts in the subject area.

In the above example, you should point out the difficulties with this approach, and suggest an alternative that is more likely to help to solve the current problems. Any one of the ideas below will work.

- Use the workshop to gather current problems, and to look at the causes of these.
- Present the manager's list of known problems to the group, and ask the group to annotate the list, adding or subtracting problems. Then present the manager's view about what is causing the problems, and what the remedy is. Ask the participants to comment on this view and to come up with any alternative or complementary causes and solutions.
- Use the workshop to focus on communication amongst senior technical staff. Begin the workshop by explaining why the Operations Manager wants to improve communication. Gather views on what is going well, what is not going well, and what changes could be made.

Question 2

The facilitator was behaving in an extremely active fashion. She bypassed the group by coming up with an initial list, and then failed to involve them all in the discussion. She needs to learn to trust the participants to come up with the ideas, as they are the subject experts. She would also benefit from learning how to use her energetic style to stimulate the group to talk and discuss, and often moves too fast through the workshop, leaving behind those who need time to reflect. Thinking time must be made available. Round robin techniques (going round the group, asking each person for a contribution) are good for including everyone, as are techniques that involve splitting the large group into smaller groups.

For the next workshop, she should follow the structure below.

- Ask the group to volunteer system requirements under a number of prepared headings (involve everyone).
- Split the group into small groups to discuss the relative merits of the requirements listed under a particular heading. Ask the group to add any other requirements that come to mind. Get each group to select their five most important and five least important system requirements.
- Take group reports and hold an open discussion of priorities.
- Vote to indicate essential and non-essential requirements.

The psychology of groups

Question 1

This is a difficult situation. The presence of a domineering boss will certainly hamper the chances of the workshop being open and honest. However, if the boss insists on being present, you have to let him know what effect his presence will have, and then give him some choices. If he has expressed a strong desire to be present, it is unlikely that he will agree to miss the workshop completely. There are therefore two possible solutions.

The first solution is to ask the boss to attend the first ten minutes and then the last half-hour of the workshop. He should be present at the start to kick things off and at the end to hear the views of the group. The boss's contribution at the end of a workshop is crucial. He will have to be primed to make encouraging noises rather than to dismiss the group's work. In my experience a domineering manager can inadvertently dismiss an entire workshop by saying 'That's all a bit obvious' or 'I'm a bit disappointed at the level of your comments' or worse 'I don't agree with any of that'. This happens more often than you might expect, and can be very deflating, and irritating for the participants. It can ruin the work of a day, shattering the commitment of those present.

The second solution is to allow him to be present throughout, but to set firm ground rules about listening to each other and sharing airtime. Use of secret suggestion, small group work and secret voting will enable participants to air their views without exposing themselves. Again, a domineering manager has to be primed on how to behave in a way that will draw participants out, rather than make them defensive.

Question 2

This set-up has tremendous potential for success. The possible advantages of this scenario are listed below.

- The mix of people will create a lively and diverse atmosphere.
- There will be very few established norms in this diverse group, so ground rules can easily be set in the workshop.
- The established consultative approach means that participants will be prepared to contribute because they know that their views are normally listened to.
- Most people will be looking forward to the workshop interaction because e-mail lacks the depth and warmth of face to face contact.

The possible disadvantages and potential pitfalls, however, are as follows.

- People who work out in the field or in small satellite offices develop cultures and norms of their own, which can sometimes lead to intransigence when they are faced with other cultures and norms.
- People from widely different backgrounds are all interested in different things. It may be difficult to keep all participants involved and stimulated.
- The participants may get drawn into leadership struggles if the workshop stretches to a day.
- Field staff may work most of the time as lone sharks, so may be rusty in the area of listening and compromise.

Success can be maximized if the following guidelines are followed.

- Give participants time to introduce themselves, and therefore to assess each other; leadership struggles can then be sorted out as soon as possible.

- Set clear workshop ground rules.
- Plan a stimulating and involving workshop in which everyone is kept busy.
- Give participants time to talk and interact, but make it constructive.

Planning a facilitated workshop

Question 1

The first aim is too vague. Which strategy are we taking about, and what are 'strategic thoughts'? A better, clearer aim might be:

> This workshop aims to bring all Business Managers in the company together to discuss and prioritize a set of company-wide sales and operations goals for the coming two years.

The second and third aims are both quite clear.

Question 2

It is not a good idea to exclude people from a workshop if their commitment is required to implement workshop recommendations. If the managers referred to above can be bypassed without affecting the success of this initiative, then there is no problem. However, if they manage the shop floor staff, their commitment to and approval of any new process will undoubtedly be required.

It might also be wise to check if the managers are really out of touch. Maybe they do have something useful to contribute.

Question 3

It depends how much time you have, how smart you are and if you have knowledge of any closely related fields. If the workshop is next week, then you have to say 'no'. A facilitator with no working knowledge of the subject area is not good value. However, if there is time to read up on the subject area, and you have some previous knowledge of connected areas, then you may stand a chance of facilitating effectively.

Question 4

This workshop design will not work. The subject matter is complex, and the participant group will be demanding. This workshop structure forces the group to whittle down their ideas before they have been fully explored. The tasks are too facile, and the workshop is too short.

The workshop aim of deciding on a business strategy is an ambitious one, which may actually be too complex for a group of ten people. A set of prioritized broad strategic goals could probably be drawn up, but the final decision would have to be made by a smaller group.

The half-day format is completely inadequate. Two days is more realistic for thrashing out all the ramifications of company strategy. External information about competitors and markets will also have to be considered. The strategy discussion should be more divergent than is allowed for in the above design. Many sources of information need to be considered and discussed before the group can begin to converge on strategic goals.

A workshop with ten management consultants together in one room will be exciting, lively and potentially explosive. Management consultants are likely to be opinionated and active, but because of their lack of practice at being members of permanent work groups, they may not be that good at listening and sharing airtime. The participants will need lots of constructive discussion and well prescribed tasks to keep them focused and to give them the kind of stimulating interaction they need. Because they do not meet very often, they will have a lot to say to each other, so the workshop needs to allow for that. Time will also need to be carefully managed.

Question 5

The design below is a half-day session, which allows the recruitment agency staff first to air their concerns, and then to decide what to do about the problems. The first part of the morning is about gathering data, and the second half is about coming up with solutions. The last part of the workshop, which involves everyone looking at everyone else's ideas, is quite an effective technique. It helps people to put their own views in perspective before giving their final votes.

Question 6

The strengths of this agenda are:

- it's brief;
- it's direct;
- it mentions the topic.

153

Getting views on home-working

Workshop Design

	Time and activity	Duration	Who
9.00	**Welcome. Explain background to workshop. Introduce workshop aims. Introduction – Finish this sentence 'I think home-working will be …' Ask everyone for a contribution and discuss each one at the top level (not in detail).** ● **Write key points raised on the flipchart.**	**30 mins**	**Full group**
	Balance sheet exercise. First, split group into twos. Ask each two to think of ten pros and ten cons of home-working.	**15 mins**	**Pairs**
	Bring everyone back together and ask each two for one pro and one con until all are listed on the balance sheet. Explain that these data will be returned to later.	**15 mins**	**Full group**
10.00	**Brainstorm key tasks of those present. Go back over brainstorm to clarify what is meant.**	**20 mins**	**Full group**
	Split into groups of three. Each group examines one section of the brainstorm, taking each item to see how it will be affected by home-working. Bring the significant implications of home-working back to the plenary group.	**40 mins**	**Threes**
11.00	**COFFEE**		
11.15	**Gather ideas together, adding the new information to the list created already.**	**15 mins**	**Full group**
11.30	**Ask the group to go back into the same threes and to look at the full list of disadvantages of the home-working scheme. Ask each group to list the resource and process changes that will have to happen to ensure that home-working succeeds. Groups then present**	**60 mins**	**Threes**

	this list back to the main group via a three-minute talk, identifying key points.		
12.30	Allow people to move around, reading each other's lists, ticking items that they agree with particularly strongly. Each person has ten ticks. Only one tick per person per item.	15 mins	Full group
	Summary and recap.	15 mins	Full group
13.00	CLOSE		

However, there are also weaknesses.

- It mentions that leadership is lacking, but gives no clues as to where, and in what way.
- The whole tone is a little threatening, and participants might arrive ready to defend themselves, rather than full of good ideas for improvement.
- Because there is no timed agenda, participants do not know what will be discussed and have no framework for thinking about how leadership can be improved.

Running a facilitated workshop

Question 1

Many facilitators carry flipchart paper, flipchart pens and tape for just this eventuality.

If you are not suitably prepared, you can use a blank side on the overhead projector to capture comments, but it will be smudgy and hot, and you will probably get a headache from staring at the projector light. Blackboards and whiteboards will do, but remember to capture all the data before you wipe them clean!

Question 2

You should let this person know that the workshop is for participants only, and observers are not encouraged. Explain that observers can affect the openness and honesty of the workshop participants.

The best thing to do if the person is insistent is to find out why he or she wants to observe, and make a judgement about whether this will have a detrimental effect on the workshop or not.

Question 3

Facilitator: 'In what way is the company mean-minded and mealy-mouthed?'
or
Facilitator: 'Can you expand on that for us please?'
or
Facilitator: 'What do you mean by that?'

Question 4

Facilitator: 'Utter rubbish? That's quite damning. I'm interested to know what makes you think that.'
or
Facilitator: 'You obviously feel very strongly about this. I'd like to know why you can't use what they have produced.'

Question 5

This can be very annoying, especially if you have spent a lot of energy planning the workshop to fit the time available. Resist the temptation to explode.

Your first move is to try to persuade them to stay by explaining the benefits to everyone of their involvement in all stages of the workshop. If they do have to go, make sure they understand that any decisions due to be made during the workshop will have to be made in their absence and without their approval. Likewise, the workshop report will only summarize what is said within the workshop. If they miss important bits, their views cannot be simply bolted on later as they will have missed essential parts of the discussion.

Question 6

Ask them to keep what they have done for later discussion, as it is useful stuff. Explain why you want them to change their focus now, in terms of the progression of the workshop, and ask them to consider Bilvo's own unique company characteristics for the remaining ten minutes.

Question 7

Quietly ask something like 'Are you OK with this exercise?' It's best to do this crouching down, so that your eyes are at the same level as hers. Leave a pause. If she is just thinking, she will tell you. If she is stuck, she will probably say so. If she has some other problem, with the question, or with the workshop, or with something completely unrelated to the workshop, she may or may not say so, but you will be able to tell if there is a serious problem from her reaction. If this type of behaviour continues, you should talk to her privately in the break to see if anything can be done, and if it cannot, recommend that she leaves the workshop.

Question 8

This key user is obviously bored, and needs to be more involved in what is going on. If you fail to involve him, you will fail to get his comments and suggestions. You could do one of the following to remedy the situation.

- Ask him a direct question about the system.
- Get him to move in closer to the screen.
- Ask him to do the typing for the demo, under your instruction (this might be risky if the system is not fail-safe).
- Give everyone an involving task, eg listing their criticisms, suggestions and questions as the demo progresses.

Question 9

It is best to address a problem like this directly. Ask the two errant participants to share their list with the rest of the group, by reading out the top two entries, for example. Explain that the whole group will benefit if all the ideas are shared openly and ask them to respect the other group members by listening to their views.

Split the two participants up in the next small group exercise to encourage them to integrate with the full group more effectively.

Question 10

Run through a summary of what has been said during the workshop, and what has been decided. Ask the group if that seems an accurate record of the workshop. If the two Business Managers do not contribute at that point, then ask them directly about their concerns.
Facilitator: 'You are both looking concerned over there. What is the problem?'

The workshop environment

Question 1

Explain to your boss that the workshop will be more effective if the participants can concentrate on the topic, and become fully involved in the discussion. If participants come and go at irregular intervals, the workshop becomes disjointed and unfocused. If you have a formal break every 90 minutes or so for 15 minutes, this should give adequate access to other parties.

My opinion is that those not attending the workshop should be encouraged to manage without the participants for as long as possible. Experience shows that so-called 'urgent' calls are rarely urgent. If your workshop is interesting and involving, participants will thank you for shielding them from unnecessary interruptions.

Question 2

The best solution is to push the small tables to the walls, and use them later on for group work. Arrange 17 seats (don't forget yourself!) in a horseshoe or a circle for the opening full group discussion. Make sure everyone can see the flipchart, whiteboard or overhead projector screen. The only drawback with this arrangement is that participants may feel awkward and exposed at the start of the workshop, because of the lack of table to hide behind!

You could push some of the small round tables together, but seating then becomes complicated and people will probably not be able to see each other's eyes. This means that communication between participants will suffer.

Question 3

If the antagonistic participant carries on sitting at the opposite end of the table from you, you will carry on getting antagonistic comments. Ideally, as the workshop progresses, this person will form allegiances with supporters of the new development, and begin to see its potential benefits. To enable this to happen, and to get this person moving around, ask people to work in pairs quite early on. However, you still have the problem later on, when the person moves back to his seat.

A better, but more devious move is to place a flipchart behind him, and ask him to move to another position around the table so that he can see the flipchart.

What to do afterwards

Question 1

The results of a brainstorming session should certainly not be reported verbatim. The brainstorm only serves to generate topics for discussion. The best policy is to report the results of the discussion that follows the brainstorm. Entries in the list of ideas may have to be paraphrased to help the readers of the report understand what was meant.

The facilitator should indicate whether voting was open or secret. This helps the reader to understand the influences acting on each individual at the time of voting.

Personal views should generally be resisted, unless the facilitator thinks his or her views give the reader access to important information that would otherwise be lost. The facilitator should only include his or her views if they add to the value of the report by giving objective information, rather than subjective opinion. If the facilitator does give his or her views in the report, this should be indicated very clearly, separating the views of the facilitator from the views of the participants.

Question 2

No one would ever write such a poor report! This report intentionally combines several problems that occur regularly with workshop reports, so serves to illustrate some important points. The main problems with the report are listed below together with ideas for rectifying each problem.

- The first paragraph gives a biased report of the initial discussion. No objective information is given. See Example A in Chapter 6 for an illustration of how a discussion can be reported objectively.
- There is no mention of when the workshop ran, and for how long. This may be significant, and should be covered early on in the report.
- The participant information given is not relevant. The telephone extension numbers and staff numbers are of little use. Jobs, locations and years of service might be more useful.
- In the first paragraph after the staff list, the text indicates that the facilitator tried to persuade the group that changes to the appraisal system were necessary. The phrase 'Most participants agreed' indicates that a persuasive tack was being used. This is manipulative and possibly counter-productive. Maybe no changes are desired at all!

- The initial brainstorm list can be left out as it serves no useful purpose. The second list needs paraphrasing (eg what does 'Manager' mean in this context?). The participant scores should be added together to show clear weightings. Incidentally, it is unusual to allow a participant to allocate more than five points per choice (one participant allocates ten points to one choice which rather skews the voting).
- The personal information about Tim and Hilary is far too subjective, and probably breaches confidentiality agreements. The facilitator seems to be telling the reader to discount the views of Tim and Hilary, but without giving us a good reason to do so. This part should be more clearly thought out, backed up with fact and explicitly labelled as presenting the views of the facilitator.
- The final discussion should be reported. It is glossed over.
- The full list of suggestions, with indications of relative importance, should be fully reported.

Question 3

I hope no one ever produces such a sketchy and ambiguous report in real life, but it serves to illustrate some significant points.

You would probably be quite confused and irritated on receiving this report. What are you supposed to do as a result of this workshop? It is not at all clear whether any decisions were made as a result of this workshop. What specifically was being reviewed? Were any changes agreed? Who were the seven users? Why were only three of them taking part? Which participants were key users?

Things could have been handled differently if a formal decision making process had been in place, for instance taking an 80 per cent 'yes' response as a clear 'yes'. This would have perhaps encouraged the other four users to take part in the workshop, and to make their views known.

Special case workshops

Question 1

There are a few things to ask before you even agree to do this workshop:

- Why do this workshop now? Why is the subject of 'Values' of interest at the moment?

- Where has the idea come from? Is it supported by the rest of the Management Board?
- What will happen to the set of values derived? Will this translate into action?
- Why two days? This seems a long time for a Management Board to be sitting still in a fast moving industry.
- Are there other burning issues that need to be tackled? Perhaps values could be derived by looking at real issues from the past, present and future.

There are two highly concerning areas in this scenario. Firstly, it is very unlikely that the Management Board members of a telecommunications company will be willing to focus on values alone for two days. It's just not meaty enough. Typically, a two-day workshop would cover vision, values and strategy rather than values alone. Secondly, the remark about the Operations Director sounds like a score to be settled rather than a business-oriented issue. Beware of the sponsor's motives.

Interview each Management Board member fairly briefly to tease out the problems and challenges facing them. You might then find yourself going back to your sponsor with an alternative agenda for the two days.

Question 2

This workshop sounds like a challenge. If the UK Team Manager sees the French as uncooperative, how do the French see the UK Team Manager? Perhaps the workshop should be about developing cross-channel teamwork, using the planning task as a vehicle to achieve this.

It is worth explaining to your sponsor that a workshop cannot 'align' people. Make sure your sponsor recognizes that he will have to listen to and try to understand all participant views. Otherwise he may end up with a worse cross-channel situation on his hands than he had before the workshop ie less alignment and less cooperation.

Questions to ask include:

- How well do team members know each other? Would time spent on introductions and updating be well spent?
- How much time will there be in total? Recommend two days with some socializing in between. One day would be too short to build a plan unless a lot of up-front work has been done.
- How does the joint planning process normally work? What level of consultation is intended? Are there already some fixed goals and objectives?

- Is this workshop going to focus on the 'what?' or the 'how?' Get the sponsor to think through what he expects participants to be discussing eg broad goals or specific tactics?
- What are the problems and challenges facing the team at present, internally and externally? Start from their current situation.
- What will be the workshop output?
- Will the workshop be run in English or French? Will there be any language difficulties?

Interview a selection of team members from both France and the United Kingdom to find out how they see their current issues and what plan they already have in place. Then you can structure the workshop around the following elements in the right proportion:

- getting to know each other;
- improving teamwork – what needs to get better?;
- achieving a shared understanding of the problems and challenges facing the team;
- setting priorities;
- building a plan for the next two years;
- sequencing and committing to actions;
- monitoring and reviewing the plan – how?

It is worth noticing that the UK Team Manager has chosen his old friend to facilitate. What are the ramifications? You may be seen to represent the UK's view (unless by some happy accident you are French). You could counteract the negative effects of this by doing one of the following:

- co-facilitating with the French team's recommended facilitator (complicated?);
- holding the event in France to give the French more ownership, and to allow them to show you around their home base;
- giving the most senior French team member a clear say in the agenda setting process.

References

Argyris, C (1992) *On Organizational Learning*, Blackwell, Oxford

Binney, G (1992) *Making Quality Work*, EIU, London

Hofstede, G (1996) *Cultures and Organizations*, McGraw-Hill, New York

Kolb, D (1984) *Experiential Learning*, Prentice Hall, Englewood Cliffs, New Jersey

Pedler, M, Burgoyne, J and Boydell, T (1996) *The Learning Company*, McGraw-Hill, New York

Index

NB: *Italics* refer to figures in the text